YOUR GUIDE TO FEELING LIGHTE
THE DREAMS OF YOU

CONNECTING TO YOUR INNER LIGHT

For Jane,
Thanks for all your
friendship & support.
Always follow your
beautiful inner light.
With love,
Christoph.
30-11-09

CHRISTOPH SPIESSENS

First Published in Great Britain in 2009 by
Ankh Mind Body Spirit Centre Ltd.

The material contained in this book is expressed in good faith for general guidance, and no liability can be accepted for loss or expense incurred as a result of relying in particular circumstances on statements made here. Under no circumstances can you hold Christoph Spiessens liable for any actions that you take as a result of reading this book. The information contained within it is not a substitute for professional advice such as that given by a medical doctor, psychiatrist, or counsellor. The information provided by Christoph Spiessens does not constitute legal or professional advice, nor does it intend to do so.

A CIP Catalogue of this book is available from
the British Library

ISBN: 978-0-956-4039-0-2

CHANDLER®
BOOK DESIGN

Typeset in Gill Sans Light 11.5pt
by Chandler Book Design,
www.chandlerbookdesign.co.uk

Printed in Great Britain by the
MPG Books Group, Bodmin and King's Lynn.

This book is dedicated to Ellen, my beautiful godchild, and to Jules, my late grandad, who always believed in me, no matter what.

Just felt like signing it once again!

Love,

Chris

Certain people, certain circumstances, certain events, certain means, and certain ideas will show up in your life, and we humans will call them "good" or "bad". But they are merely like the dots in a children's book that need connecting to reveal the image. How fast you connect those dots is up to you. Occasionally some dots will be missing and you'll need to be creative and add your own.

The more consciously you connect all the dots that appear in your life, the more you will recognise the pattern, and in time be amazed by the magnificent design your soul has in mind for you.

Connecting to Your Inner Light

Your Guide to Feeling Lighter and Following the Dreams of Your Soul

---

Christoph Spiessens, CTACC

Founder of Ankh Mind Body Spirit Centre Ltd.

www.ankhcentre.com
info@ankhcentre.com

www.ChristophSpiessens.com

Contents

Acknowledgements

My grateful thanks to Gerda, Steven, Kiran, Abkar, the Friends of Ankh Mind Body Spirit Centre, my parents, Richard, George, Geeta, Kirsty, Tania, Val, my spiritual teachers, and the Universe.

Thank you for helping me to manifest my first book.

Thanks for helping me spread my wings.

A special "thank you" to all my coaching clients, Reiki students and the lovely people who have attended my seminars and workshops. Your kind words, positive feedback, encouragement and energy are much appreciated.

Foreword

by Val Cunningham, Principal of the UK School of Mediumship

Connecting to Your Inner Light is a wonderfully inspiring book, offering easy to follow steps towards peace, joy and self discovery. Gifted in his spiritual approach to life, Christoph guides you to connect with your soul, love yourself more, and live a life of light and happiness.

Don't just take my word for it; discover for yourself the beautifully accessible and gentle guidance within. Christoph's gifts as a Spiritual Life Coach are outstanding and this book is a gift for your soul and an essential read for those awakening to their own Inner Light.

This wonderful book is about Life; it is about Love; and it is about You. It is a book we all need to read. This is a book to change your life.

Val Cunningham MSc MA BA (1st) hons

Val is a Public Speaker & Seminar Presenter on Spirituality & Mediumship and is the Principal of the UK School of Mediumship. www.valcunninghaminternational.com

Introduction

Dear Friend,

This book is about you. It will help you to bring more joy and happiness into your life. It's designed to be a guide that you can use whenever you look for inspiration and guidance. ***Connecting to Your Inner Light*** is a collection of insights and powerful tips that I use in my own life and with my coaching clients during private sessions, workshops and group seminars.

It can be challenging to find the time to read an entire book on self-improvement and spiritual growth. Sometimes all we long for is a quick boost of confidence or feeling of self-worth, something uplifting that gives us the strength and motivation to move forward in life. Let this book be your guide. When you are reading through this book there are exercises throughout to help you chart your progress. Your answers to the exercises can either be written directly into this book in the space provided or you may wish to have a journal with you to write your answers in.

Practical spirituality is a vital key to living a fulfilling life. It gives you the tools to understand the bigger picture and helps you make sense of all the good and challenging things that "happen" to you.

Spirituality in its most basic form means "living consciously". Spirituality has nothing to do with religion and is detached from any dogmas. It refers to being fully present and living your life with an attitude of awareness. Being spiritually aware helps people to understand what goes on in their life and, perhaps more importantly, ***why*** it goes on. It's an opportunity to explore who we really are, what the reason is for being here, and how to make the most of this phenomenal experience. It allows people to reconnect to their own values and beliefs, rather than those imposed upon them by work and society. Spirituality encourages people to move away from playing the role of victim and removes any obstacles they may have created for themselves.

Practical spirituality will lead you to the freedom for which you have been searching: freedom from guilt, anger, frustration, feeling stuck, difficult relationships, financial concerns, health issues, low self-esteem, and so forth. Freedom can be experienced through increased awareness and from being at peace with yourself. No other relationship can ever bring you as much love, understanding, support, and happiness as the relationship you have with your ***Self.*** You are the most important person in your life. Once you completely align your actions with your own values and beliefs, you will discover a wonderful sense of peace within and new possibilities and opportunities will appear as if by magic.

A useful way to enjoy the full potential of your spiritual path is by taking small steps, and that is why I have created this book. All the tips offered here will help you on your exciting journey towards more daily happiness, one accessible step at a time.

You can use this book as a quick reference guide by picking one or two topics every day. Allow yourself to reflect on the information for a couple of minutes, and listen closely to your thoughts and feelings; they are an invaluable compass. Then consider how the quality of your life could improve by putting these tips into practice.

Some tips may resonate with you more than others. No-one has the power to change you; only you can do that. But if you do like the ideas offered in this book, you really can use them to become "in tune" with yourself and your life. At times you may find you need to apply extra effort to put some of the tips into use in your life, and with others you can apply them more easily. As with anything, be patient with yourself on this journey. Allow yourself time to assimilate all the information. Think of these tips as flower seeds. In order to grow beautifully, the seeds need to push through the soil and rocky bottom. This will take time and persistence, but the result is well worth the effort. The inspirations as described in ***Connecting to Your Inner Light*** have helped to positively transform my own life and the lives of my coaching clients. They bring understanding, freedom, and true happiness. My aim with my book is to help you feel lighter and better about yourself and your life.

We are all looking for answers, but first we need to ask ourselves the ***right questions.*** This book will give you the guidance you need. Through the process of spiritual enquiry, the right questions will lead you to the right answers. When you allow miracles to happen, they will. Are you ready to let miracles into your life?

Much love,
Christoph Spiessens

Essential Information Before Reading This Book

I wanted to write a book that was accessible and would offer an introduction to practical spirituality to the newcomer, and some helpful guidance to those further along their spiritual journey. Too many unnecessarily complex books are available on the subjects of God, spiritual enquiry and personal development, and most of them are gathering dust on the shelves of bookshops and libraries.

It was an easy-to-read yet compelling book that catapulted my own spiritual development many years ago, and I would like this book to have a similar effect on you. It is not my intention to try and make you believe anything or to turn you into a spiritual guru. I'm also not looking to provoke or offend anyone. I simply felt inspired to finally write down much of the material I share in my workshops and seminars and to summarise it in a book that people could use as a quick reference guide.

I hope you enjoy reading my first book. I am confident it will provide you with lots of information that will make you think about yourself, your life, the world and the Universe on a whole new level.

Here are some key concepts that I will be delving deeper into throughout the book:

Life Coaching

A coaching session is a structured conversation between a qualified coach and a client to facilitate change. It is a co-creative process where goals, ideas and options are explored in order to guide the client forward in life. Coaching sessions can be done in person, over the phone, or by email, and are carried out individually or in a group.

Spiritual Coaching

This is a form of coaching that helps clients to further develop their interest in spirituality. Topics typically include exploring one's life purpose, restoring work-life balance, moving away from organised religion, exploring the pathways of the soul, mind-body-spirit connections, psychic awareness, developing holistic healing skills, reincarnation and Karma.

The "God" in This Book

Let's be straight here: My work does not endorse any form of organised religion, and this is ***not*** a book about God. However, I will refer to "God" on several occasions, so let me briefly explain what I mean when I mention the word ***God.*** It's quite simply the source of everything. That's why many people, including myself, prefer to call it ***All That Is,*** the ***Source, Oneness***, or the ***Universe.*** It's a form of energy that powers everything. It's not a person with a long beard or some kind of mystic creature, and it definitely doesn't sit on a throne somewhere between puffy clouds.

The Source doesn't punish you, impose barriers or make you miserable. It's the energy source from which everything once birthed. That includes you. In other words, you are a part of God and God is a part of you. Your "inner light" is the divine spark that's present within your being. It's an all-knowing consciousness and is very accessible.

All we need to understand is how to access that Source, and once you have established the connection, you will be able to live your life on a very different and exciting new level. That's precisely what this book and my coaching work are about: connecting people to their inner light. I respect people's decision to go to a place of worship to praise their God. However, the God in my work is totally detached from any religion, and the word God is used to express that incredible, loving, universal force that fuels everything and anything.

The Soul

Your soul truly is amazing. It's a form of energy that once birthed from God/the Universe/All That Is. This entity is on a self-chosen journey to perfect itself because it wants to grow and evolve, but why? A very basic explanation (I promised to keep it simple) is that the soul experiences life and feeds this data back to the God Source. Remember, you are part of that God Source, so when you are here on Earth, you learn in order to evolve your soul. You may know everything, but that doesn't mean you've ***experienced*** it, so basically you experience life so that the God Source (and, in turn, ***you***) can ***remember*** what you already knew, but now also understand what it ***feels*** like.

Your soul really is eternal and will, at some point, eventually return back into the God Source. This is where ***reincarnation*** comes in; until our soul has reached the final stages of evolving, we "choose" different things to happen to us over a variety of lifetimes. This is the very reason for living. You'll experience a great variety of both positive and challenging things in life, and all this will help your soul to learn and grow. Understanding this will give you a tremendous head start, for you will live your life with increased awareness and appreciation. Knowing that it was ***you*** (as your soul) who decided the major "lessons" you would learn while you are on this planet will empower you to deal better with life's challenges. But you will also appreciate your ***Self*** more and the good things that are already present in your life. It is far easier to make sense of your life when you understand your ***reasons*** for living it.

The subtitle of this book, ***Your Guide to Feeling Lighter and Following the Dreams of Your Soul,*** refers to living out the experiences – the dreams – you chose for yourself to experience before you were born. The basics of those dreams are stored in your inner light, and if you are reading this book now, it means that the time is right for you to receive this information. This guidance can help you connect to ***your*** inner light so that you can explore those innate dreams and live a really great, abundant and fulfilling life.

As you can imagine, this topic is so extensive that a whole collection of books could be written about it, and even that would only be scratching the surface. What I would like to offer in this book are insights and tips that you can put into practice straight away. After all, that is what practical spirituality is all about: honouring the journey of your soul by living your life the best you can.

I am honoured to be a part of your journey.

PART 1:
Inspirations for a Lighter Life

Define What You Want From Life

Parents, teachers and bosses all tend to have ideas and opinions about what you should do with your life. They ***think*** they know you, and often they have the best intentions for you and your future. However, due to this constant pressure from society, you may opt for a career/life path that's not necessarily the right one for you. It's a natural reaction; after all you are simply trying to meet other people's expectations. But what about your ***own*** expectations? What do ***you*** want from your life? The more you can define what will bring you real joy, the easier it will be to work towards it.

I suggest you don't put any stress on yourself. Some people spend so much energy on finding their life purpose they don't see the many ways in which they could make themselves useful in the meantime. We will be delving deeper into discovering your life purpose later on in this book, but for now ask yourself: What are my skills and talents? What am I naturally good at? What gives me a tremendous sense of accomplishment? What makes my heart sing?

Enjoy the process of ***discovering*** life and what you expect from it, rather than always struggling. Though life may sometimes seem a perpetual struggle it is much more than that. Life is our opportunity to evolve and grow, share, give and receive blessings, and expect miracles. Each day is a precious gift to explore and enjoy your journey.

When looking at what you want from life it is good to generalise at first and then narrow things down, following the beat of your own drum, your authentic self. For example, when I was looking for my life purpose, I said, "I want to work with people and I want to help them." That's a pretty vague statement, don't you think? Then I started to ask myself the right questions: "What does working with people look like?" "Which people?" "Helping with what?" "Where?" "How?" By answering these small but important questions, the right answers came to me. I became clear on how I could best help people and who would benefit most from the services that I offer. I discovered where and what to study so that I could expand my skills and the answers guided me to the right logistics I needed when I was setting up my coaching practice.

What do ***you*** want from life? Are you holding yourself back? Are you scared that following your passion may not necessarily make you a multi-millionaire? How will you know if you don't try? Are any limiting beliefs holding you back when your heart is crying out to express your innate talents?

There is a light within you. That light is your truth, your ***essence***. It always shines but sometimes appears less bright due to stress and pressure caused by society, but often also by ***ourselves***. Go and find your light. It will illuminate your path.

To go high up in life,
go deep down in your heart.

Believe in Yourself!

During a coaching session, a client, whom I'll call Sarah, once told me she felt very frustrated about the fact that nobody seemed to believe in her. Sarah wanted to become a playwright but had so far been "unsuccessful", an opinion that she based entirely on not having been hired by a theatre company yet.

She ***assumed*** that she was simply not "good" enough. Competition was tough, and she had limited time available to write since she was working full-time to support her family. Sarah was seriously beginning to doubt her writing talents and had thought about giving up. "Can you know for sure that a series of unsuccessful writing proposals equals a lack of talent on your behalf?" I asked.

She thought hard about this. "No," she said, "I can't know that for sure."

"But it does affect my self-confidence." She added.

"Does that mean that people need to believe in you first in order for you to believe in yourself?" I asked.

She immediately understood what I meant. And with that came the realisation that her entire image of self-worth and self-confidence had been depending on other people and their (often unjustified) opinions.

"How can you turn this around?" I asked her.

"I need to believe in myself first."

"How will you do that?"

"I will envision people enjoying my work. I accept the ride might be bumpy, but I know that I am good at this and I know that I can do it."

"So, the image that you have of yourself will be created by whom?"

"Entirely by myself."

A few weeks later Sarah secured her first writing contract with a local theatre company.

When you feel disempowered or not believed in, it means you have given your personal power away to other people. You no longer feel self-empowered. Yes, we all like to be valued and appreciated, but please don't let your sense of self-worth depend entirely on others. Relying on others to make you feel better about who you are can make you appear weak in their eyes. After all you are handing them your power to decide what you should think of yourself.

Love yourself first. If **you** don't believe in yourself and what you have to offer, how can you expect other people to believe in you?

Question to ask yourself: Do I really believe in myself?

If not, go deeper:

- ***"Who would I be if I was more self-confident?"***
- ***"What could I achieve if only I believed in myself more?"***
- ***"Which small step can I make today to take back my power?"***

And you will see that, as always, asking yourself the right questions will bring you the right answers.

Love Yourself, and Others Will Follow You

Self-love is not the same as vanity or conceit. Loving yourself means appreciating the miracle that you are and honouring your mind, body and soul.

If you respect yourself for whom and what you are, with all your incredible talents and capacities, you will be strong enough to spend time on your own and live with confidence. Your happiness will no longer depend on other people and their opinions. Does the way you see yourself depend too much on what people tell you? Have a couple of unpleasant job interviews or other confrontations and experiences made you believe that you are not good enough, not talented enough, to do what you want to do?

Trust me when I say this: ***You are perfect in every way.*** Even if it doesn't always feel that way, you really are. The situation you are in may not always make you feel good, but ***your soul is always pure and perfect***. It's an integral part of the Universe and therefore cannot be diminished.

When you begin to truly appreciate yourself, you will radiate self-respect and confidence. It will be so powerful that it will make people curious and you will attract their attention. They will want to know your secret. And if they don't understand your optimism and love for yourself and your life, that's fine too. Your sense of self-worth doesn't depend on what others reflect back to you.

We are all souls born from the Source (Universe, God, All That Is), deserving every good in life, including taking off at least one day of the weekend to smell the roses, rest and relax, and have fun. Everything starts at home, but the most important thing is to love ourselves. When we love ourselves, we almost magically develop love for others, and people respond in a favourable way to us.

I am perfect because I am part of the Universe.

You Always Have a Choice: From Victim to Winner in Your Life!

If I told you that about 90 percent of all the things that happen to you in your life—good and bad—are caused by you, you will most likely not believe me. You would tell me: "I didn't want to get that divorce" or "I didn't want to lose my job and my house" or "I certainly didn't want to see my business go bankrupt" or even "I didn't plan to win the lottery". However, you experience your life on Earth (and on many other planets) in order to perfect your soul. That soul, once born from the Source, "picks" certain situations it wants to experience when it takes on the human form.

You ***are*** your soul in this lifetime but you are not your whole soul. Your soul is so multi-dimensional it would be impossible to understand it completely in this lifetime. It's important to remember, however, that we should take responsibility for everything we do in life, for we "choose" these experiences to happen. Good or bad, we co-create our whole life. You could say that the Universe has a catalogue of experiences from which your soul can choose before it incarnates, and during your time on Earth, you have an ***opportunity, not a duty,*** to undergo these experiences. The more you can do this, the more your soul learns and grows. This is what ***Karma*** is about: learning experiences for the soul. And you can take as many lifetimes as necessary to fill in these pieces of Karma until you get it "right".

I really believe this is true. It gives me so much ***freedom.*** You may say, "Wait a minute! If everything is already decided for me, why should I bother working hard? Why even make an effort?"

Let me tell you, you don't ***have*** to! You have an ***opportunity*** to do so if you wish, but you also have ***free will*** and so the ***choice*** is yours. You have choice to assist in your soul's growth, or you can put it on hold for a while, because no matter what, you will still be evolving.

Now that you know this, why not take advantage and make the most of it? Understanding the reason why you experience all the heartaches, financial worries, relationship issues, confusion, despair, but also joy, prosperity, abundance and extreme wealth, really gives you a huge head start!

You are incredibly powerful. You really do have a choice**. *Always!*** Regardless of what happens in your life you always have the freedom to choose your attitude.

Have you ever considered this? Let's say you have just been fired. Whether you accept that this experience may be something your soul wanted to learn or not, you are empowered to decide how you will ***feel*** about it. Will it take you a week or six months to come to terms with it? ***You*** decide!

I am not suggesting suppressing your feelings (which is very harmful), what I am talking about is to know when enough is enough. So many people seem to be stuck in the "victim role". They let their entire happiness and wellbeing depend on other people.

Be smart, choose to feel ***great*** about your life and all its ups and "downs"!

Questions to ask yourself: Am I the victim of my life? Do I always feel sorry for myself?

Now meditate on the idea that your life could be a lot lighter, and all you need to do is to choose to feel good.

As always, be gentle on yourself. Move from victim to winner in your own life!

Life is a like visit to the library.

Making the trip to the library and enjoying the atmosphere does not mean you have to read every book you'll find there.
But you could. If you wanted to. The choice is yours alone.
There is no book you have to read.

But there might be something on the shelves that's rather special.

Dare to pick up the book.
Or save it for another visit.

Stop All Negative Thinking

Negative thinking destroys the way you view yourself and the world. It limits your creativity. It keeps doors closed. It makes you feel sad. And by the ***universal law of attraction,*** stating that like attracts like, negative thinking will attract more negativity into your life.

What causes us to think negatively? It happens when we can't deal with the challenges in our life in a balanced way. Negative thinking occurs when we block ourselves from looking at how we can overcome difficulties in a constructive manner.

Often people seem trapped in a vicious circle. They experience something bad and can no longer keep themselves motivated. They lose the strength to carry on, become disillusioned and don't know how they could possibly begin to change their life.

Know that your past doesn't have to equal your future. There is always a way to turn things around. The question is how willing are you to allow this to happen? Sometimes the negative circumstances in which people find themselves almost become their "comfort zone" and it can be a little bit challenging to leave your comfort zone.

As more and more scientific proof becomes available about how negative thinking can cause diseases in our bodies, it is very important to learn how we can turn this negative thinking around.

Whenever I find myself thinking negatively, here's what I do and it really works: I immediately come up with an alternative thought. I literally replace the old thought with a new one. This does not necessarily mean that what I think is true or will become true. What matters is that I can quickly shift my thinking from bad to positive, from something that makes me feel bad to something that makes me feel better about a particular situation. Try it for yourself—you will see.

Questions to ask yourself: Am I trapped in my own negative thinking? What good has ever come from my it?

For more information on how to create loving and powerful thoughts, please refer to "Use Positive Affirmations".

If every thought creates your future, you might want to think twice.

Use Positive Affirmations

Affirmations are ***power thoughts*** we have about ourselves and our world that make us feel a certain way. Creating your own positive affirmations is a great and fun way to build your self-confidence and to calm your mind instantly. Did you know that we use affirmations all the time? The problem, however, is that we are mostly unaware of it. Moreover, most of the time, our power thoughts are destructive and therefore they will undermine our self-image.

Do the following negative affirmations sound familiar to you?

- ***"I'm not good enough."***
- ***"I could never do that."***
- ***"I am not strong enough."***
- ***"I don't have enough money to try that."***
- ***"I look tired."***
- ***"I'm not smart enough to do that."***

Negative affirmations are having a great time in your mind. Sometimes they seem to multiply by the minute! They have the power to make you feel worthless and weak because they generate bad feelings about yourself and your world. Remember, what we focus on we attract more of.

Question to ask yourself: How good would it be to have more positive thoughts in my mind?

With a little bit of practice, you ***can*** achieve that. All that is needed is to know ***how*** to create power thoughts that will work for you.

Positive affirmations should be:

- ***Uplifting (be creative and use positive language)***
- ***First person – start them with "I" or "My" (to reinforce your power and control)***
- ***Easy to remember (the more you use them, the better)***

For example:

- If you are nervous when going to a party, no longer think, "People will think I look tired" or "They will see me as an underachiever". Instead, replace the negative affirmation with a positive one: "I look good and people like me."
- If you wake up dreading the day ahead, think: "I am healthy and I am enjoying this day already!"
- When you feel stressed and overworked try: "I admire myself and my ability to multitask."

Positive affirmations are the foundation of a healthy self-image. I use them for myself all the time and show my coaching clients how they can easily create their own. These loving thoughts about yourself and your world can change any state from bad to good immediately.

Here are some more positive affirmations to inspire you:

- ***"I am a great listener."***
- ***"I have so much to offer to the world."***
- ***"My life blossoms every day."***
- ***"My talents inspire others."***

- ***"I feel good and I am loved."***
- ***"I am safe and guided by the Universe."***
- ***"My input is valuable."***
- ***"My body is strong and healthy."***
- ***"I attract love easily."***
- ***"I am appreciated by many."***
- ***"I love and I am loved."***
- ***"I always do a great job."***
- ***"What I need comes to me."***
- ***"I know what to do and when."***
- ***"I am proud of all my accomplishments."***
- ***"I am free to be ME!"***

When you wake up in the morning there are always a couple of seconds when everything is blissful and calm, just before the conscious mind kicks in. You know what I'm talking about, right? Before the tape in your head starts to play again and before the negative chatter begins I find it extremely helpful to use a positive affirmation during those vital first seconds of my day. As soon as I open my eyes, before any other thoughts enter my mind, I say, "All is well and I am loved." I swear by it, for it literally programmes me for the day ahead.

Question to ask yourself below or in your journal: What is the first thing I would like to tell myself in the morning?

My answer:

____

____

____

____

Now create your loving "morning" affirmation below or in your journal. Remember to begin with "I" or "My" and use positive words, keeping it short and sweet.

My morning affirmation:

____

____

____

____

A note about affirmations: They are an invaluable tool to enhance your self-image, but they are not a substitute for professional help for certain emotional or mental conditions. You can compare them with vitamin tablets; their beneficial effects have been proven, but they can only enhance your diet, not replace it.

Listen to the Voice Within

The voice within is not one of those voices in your head. It's the voice of your soul. Before you were born in this lifetime, your soul decided on the path it would take during your life on Earth. That means that your soul, in many ways, knows what lies ahead of you. Sometimes you will need to make certain decisions or moves, and that's when the voice within becomes a wonderful source of information.

The voice within truly is a spiritual compass; it will always show you the right direction. The biggest challenge, however, is learning to ***trust*** the guidance. Very often we are conditioned by society to think rationally, rather than emotionally. That's why many people find it difficult to listen to this inner guidance. When external pressure is too high, the internal help is suppressed.

Question to ask yourself: Do I allow myself to listen to my inner voice?

Here are some of the reasons why people may find it difficult to trust their heart's guidance:

- Peer pressure to follow the crowd
- A past experience with an unsatisfactory result
- Financial reasons
- Not used to making their own decisions
- Out of touch with their emotions

- No encouragement from friends and family/high expectations from parents

Do any of these reasons sound familiar to you? Learning to trust your inner guidance can take time and works best when you keep out negative influences from around you. Everyone can do this, but it will take a little practice.

Let's revisit the fears behind listening to your inner voice and how you can overcome them:

- **Peer pressure to follow the crowd.** Is blindly following the crowd really worth your time and energy? Are you always nodding "yes" when your heart is saying "no"? What's the point in going with the masses? If you like what your inner guidance is telling you, trust it, embrace it and act upon it. Stand up for your beliefs and use the opportunity to spread your wings. And remember: ***It's good to be different!***

- **A past experience with an unsatisfactory result.** Maybe you had a bolt of inspiration in the past and you decided to follow it through. However, due to circumstances, your idea didn't turn out to be as "successful" as you had hoped. I can understand why that may have left you feeling disappointed at one time, but the past doesn't have to equal the future. It's a shame how so many people beat themselves up all the time, cursing the things they've done "wrong" in the past or (worse still) worrying about everything they didn't do but maybe should have done. I suggest you look back on your perceived "failure" and appreciate the insight and experience you've gained from it. In those cases, your inner guidance didn't lead you astray; it was simply one of the many lessons we learn in life, nothing more and nothing less. Or maybe you can fine-tune your inner guidance a little and look deeper, reflect on it, and only go ahead when you feel happy with the direction your heart's compass indicates.

- **Financial reasons.** I truly know and believe that the Universe supports us in many wonderful ways. If you have a dream and the world will benefit from it, you can be sure that the right means will come to you, sooner or later. Worrying about the financial side of your creative projects can hinder the process of realising your dreams. Remember, we cannot build the roof without making sure the walls are in place first. I am sure that, whatever your vision might be, there are things you can do ***today*** that don't require any financial investment. Get the ball rolling. Even if it's simply thinking out loud about how successful your project will be. Remember that your thoughts are powerful, for they inspire you to take action, which brings results. Listen to the voice within and trust its guidance will bring to you the money needed to realise your ambitions. When you are happy, your energy begins to shift to a higher vibration, which makes it easier for the Universe to send money your way. It's difficult to attract money when your mind is preoccupied with the specifics of how that will happen. Instead focus solely on the ***joy*** you experience from working on your dreams. Give your financial concerns to the Universe, and trust that the right people, means and circumstances will come your way. You will see.

- **Not used to making their own decisions.** If you always surround yourself with people who are "louder" than you, it's likely you never have a chance to speak up for yourself and to make your own decisions. This will have a negative influence on following your intuition. Maybe you are not even aware that you have this valuable source of information within you. Next time someone else makes a decision for you, I want you to pay close attention to your feelings. In the past, you've probably already thought, "Hey, wait a minute!" when something felt awkward, but you didn't say anything because you are so used to other people telling you what to do and how you should be. Now is a perfect time to begin making your own decisions in life. You are strong enough and smart enough not having to depend on other people's opinions. The more you learn to be your own "boss", the more you'll become your own best friend as well, and the easier it will be to follow your inner compass.

- **Out of touch with their emotions.** If you have only recently started to explore yourself and your life, discovering your emotional side may be a little bit awkward. You may feel vulnerable and less in control, however your emotions are a vital key to manifesting your dreams. They reflect how well you are listening to the voice within you. Use your emotions to translate your heart's guidance. Whether you feel strongly opposed to something or you are filled with joy, become aware of your emotional reactions and begin to trust them. The more you get in touch with that side of you, the easier it will be to follow the guidance and support it offers you.

- **No encouragement from friends and family/high expectations from parents.** You will sometimes need to be "lovingly assertive" with certain members of your family and friends when it comes to following the dreams of your soul. Not all of them will be into personal growth, and they may not share your dream of having a life full of abundance and happiness either. Maybe they even display negative behaviour, which is common for people who have given up on their own dreams and aspirations. This lack of interest and encouragement can make it difficult for you to listen to your inner voice of guidance. Sometimes it may be better for you to distance yourself a bit and surround yourself with people who ***are*** on your spiritual wavelength. Don't fear being lonely; more time to yourself may be exactly what your soul needs to explore its creative desires.

The voice within you is the voice of your soul.
It is the best life coach you will ever find.

Be Excited about Being a Spiritual Person

Okay, so you're into spirituality.... Do you feel like you want to talk more about it, live it and share your passion for it? Hiding in the Mind Body Spirit section of the local bookshop or being a part of online communities is for many people as good as it gets when it comes to following their interest in spirituality. Even though the world has seen a positive spiritual revolution over recent years and the topic has become much more accessible, it seems that many people are still in the spiritual closet. This could partly be because of geographical, cultural or religious circumstances, however it seems to me that one of the main reasons is that they don't quite see yet how they could combine their interest in spirituality with everyday life. Many people seem to have spirituality in their life as some kind of hobby, something you do once all the other "important" duties have been done. But spirituality is a way of life.

Step up to your full spiritual potential and become a beacon of light. Live your essence, be authentic and lock on to your own divinity. Lead by example and offer inspiration and guidance to the many souls who are searching for the truth.

There's never been a better time to come out of the spiritual closet. People all around the world are rapidly learning about the wonderful benefits that spirituality has to offer. More and more spiritual teachers and authors are sharing their insights and helping people to significantly improve the quality of their life. If you feel the odd one out, why not tell your friends that you are really fascinated by spirituality? Sometimes people need a little help to get to understand you better. Maybe they don't always know how to approach you because the topic of spirituality might make them feel somewhat uncomfortable. Remember that many people are still under the impression that spirituality is linked to organised religion. There are, however, ways to overcome this.

Tell your friends:

- What spirituality is
- What it means to ***you***
- How it helps you
- How you want to engage in it more

Your friends and family will certainly find it helpful and probably fascinating as well. Often during a chat with them about spirituality, you will notice that they too are interested in the subject to a certain extent.

I'm going to share with you a personal explanation of spirituality. I have used it in the introduction to this book, but I want to revisit it here. It can be useful in assisting you to "help" your friends, family members or work colleagues as you explain to them what spirituality means to you.

In its most basic form spirituality means ***living consciously***. Spirituality has nothing to do with religion and is detached from any dogmas. Being spiritual refers to being fully present and living your life with an attitude of increased awareness, appreciating the flow of life for "what it is" all the while exploring your true self. Being spiritually aware helps people to understand what happens in their lives and, more importantly, ***why*** it happens. It allows people to reconnect to their own values and beliefs, rather than those imposed on them by work and society. Spirituality encourages people to move away from the role of "victim" and any blockages they have created for themselves.

Practical spirituality will lead you to the freedom you have always been seeking: freedom from guilt, anger, frustration, feelings of being stuck, difficult relationships, financial concerns, health issues, low self-esteem, and so on. Freedom can only come from being at peace with your own self. No other relationship can ever bring you as much love, understanding, support, and happiness as the relationship you have with yourself. You are the most important person in your life. Once you completely align your thoughts and actions with your own values and beliefs, you will discover a wonderful sense of peace within, and new possibilities will show up as if by magic.

Express Your Gratitude Every Day

Who do you prefer to interact with the most: people who are grateful for what you do for them or those who just can't seem to say, "Thank you"? We all like to feel respected and appreciated for what we do. Children in particular love to be rewarded when they have done something good. You feel great when your boss or your client is grateful for your efforts. Did you know it works in a very similar way for the Universe? The more grateful we are for the things in our life, the more the Universe will provide us with more of what we enjoy. By having an "attitude of gratitude" we let the Universe know that we appreciate the goodness it sends our way.

You don't need to perform any complicated ceremonies to express your gratitude to the Universe. All you need to do is to get into a habit of saying "Thank you" often. Not only will you attract more goodness into your life; you will also naturally begin to feel much better when you are in a state of gratitude and appreciation. It will also help you to realise just how much you ***already*** have in your life to be grateful for. We just need to remind ourselves sometimes.

Learning to act "as if" will help you with manifesting your wishes. I like to say, "Thank you for a safe journey" before I set off, as I have already thanked the Universe ***in advance*** for a safe trip. Try it for yourself. Envisaging a safe journey before you even leave will help you to be calm and focused. You may programme your trip via a map route or G.P.S but it is equally important to programme yourself mentally.

I go about my day saying "Thank you!" often: Thank you for the sunshine, thank you for the lovely music, thank you for the phone call from my father, thank you for the friendship I get from my cats, thank you for these great clothes, thank you for my car, thank you for the coaching seminars and lectures I get booked for, thank you for the book I'm writing. I even thank the flowers and plants in my house for their beauty. Thank you, thank you, thank you!

Being grateful and appreciative are attitudes that will really lift your spirits. What have you got to lose? Saying "Thank you!" is free! It may not always be easy, you may not always realise just how much you have got in your life to be thankful for, but it is very powerful indeed, and I recommend you get yourself into the habit of saying "Thank you!" more often.

So, start saying "Thank you" for waking up feeling refreshed after a safe night's sleep, for the hot water you can shower with, for a safe journey to work, for being an inspiration to other people, for a nice lunch, for a lovely cup of tea, for being busy at work, for that constructive feedback, for the challenges that allowed you to grow, for the eyes that enable you to see, for the beauty of the flowers, for the rain that makes those flowers grow, for the—your list is endless. Be creative with this! Thank you!

Question to ask yourself: What am I grateful for?

Clients often ask me, "Why would I be grateful for all the things that go ***wrong*** in my life?" First of all, I suggest you look at those situations as ***learning opportunities*** for your soul. If everything goes right all the time, we can be happy but would not grow spiritually as rapidly as when we do when we overcome difficulties. Secondly, concepts such as "wrong" and "right" are labels introduced by us, humans. The more you develop your spiritual side, the more you'll come to understand that everything always comes down to experience. The result of an experience may ***feel*** "right" or "wrong" but the very nature of experience is just that what it is: ***experience***.

I am especially thankful for the challenges and adversities that I face. That, my friends, is what spirituality is all about: seeing the bigger picture, getting out of the victim role ("I am so sad and poor and scared"), and living your life with passion and dedication!

Be very direct with the Universe: Say, "Thank you for this challenging time in my life, I accept the learning opportunity, and I am grateful that I have come out at the other end a stronger person." The Universe will then help you with this spiritual "assignment" and help you to move on quickly. This is where it becomes tricky for those people who seem to really "enjoy" feeling miserable. They tell the whole world about it! They bask in the attention they get from letting everybody know just how sad their situation is. They seem to be "grateful" for it. So what happens? The Universe sends more "misery" their way. It is far more effective to give thanks for having got through whatever challenge has come up (even if you're still going through the challenge), than to dwell on the misery of a problem. What we focus on we attract.

Exercise: In your journal or below name five things that you are especially grateful for in your life:

1. ______________________________

2. ______________________________

3. ______________________________

4. ______________________________

5. ______________________________

Now try 10 more!

1. ________________

2. ________________

3. ________________

4. ________________

5. ________________

6. ________________

7. ________________

8. ________________

9. ________________

10. ________________

Now try another 20!

1. ________________

2. ________________

3. ________________

4. ________________

5. ________________

6. ________________

Another 20 Continued!

7. ______________________________

8. ______________________________

9. ______________________________

10. ______________________________

11. ______________________________

12. ______________________________

13. ______________________________

14. ______________________________

15. ______________________________

16. ______________________________

17. ______________________________

18. ______________________________

19. ______________________________

20. ______________________________

I love including this powerful exercise in my workshops and coaching assignments. Taking a moment to list all the things we have to be grateful for can be a real eye-opener. It helps us realise that we spend too much time wishing for better when in fact so many wonderful things are ***already*** present in our lives. Moreover, this exercise can quickly lift your mood on a blue day.... And remember, when we adopt a gratitude attitude, we give the Universe a "green light" to send more goodness our way!

Tell People How Much They Mean to You

We often assume that people know we love them; we almost take it for granted. But do you know for sure that the people you love know that you love them? How? Do you wait for a special occasion until you thank someone or express your love? Does it make you feel uncomfortable to tell your friends how much you care about them?

Question to ask yourself: Who has been particularly helpful to me recently?

Wouldn't it be nice to let that person know? If you are a little bit nervous or don't know how to do this, find a simple way that feels comfortable for you. You could send your friend an email or a text message, give them a small present, or simply talk to them directly. You will be surprised how good it feels to say, "Thank you" and you'll know just how much they value your feedback. This is not restricted to your circle of friends, family members or work colleagues. I sometimes send an email to express my thanks to authors, artists and public speakers who have inspired me in one way or another, and I still have their reply emails on file.

At the end of a coaching session or group seminar, I always like to thank people. I let them know how much they mean to me. It doesn't take long and it is enormously appreciated by them; sometimes people are even a bit shocked. It makes them feel valued and respected.

Exercise: Get in touch with someone *now* and tell them how much you value them. Do it now!

No matter how busy your life gets, it's good to remember to make time for your special friends. They are the people who stand by you, support you and believe in you (often more than you do in yourself). The same goes for your loved one; allow some space in your diary to spend some quality time with your partner, away from stress and distractions. As we follow and realise our dreams and careers, it's easy to become overly self-absorbed and forget about our partner and friends. Sometimes we even "use" them to vent our frustrations, and they become our personal therapists when we need someone to help us carry the weight.

It's good to make that extra effort and create a healthy balance between work and our personal life. If you are a busy and successful person already, make sure to invest time in the special people in your life, because it can be lonely at the top.

Hug People

Human touch is amazing! Studies show that human touch can help boost our immune system and play a major part in the healing process.

Hug people, connect with their energy, and enjoy it all the way. Your soul longs to experience love as part of its incarnation here on Earth. The lovely feeling you get from hugging someone nourishes your soul.

When you hug another person, your aura blends in with theirs during that moment. That's a spiritual connection. Notice if you can intuitively pick up on the emotions and feelings of that person. If you feel it is appropriate, you may want to share this information with the person.

Hugging is to a soul what kissing is to humans.

If you feel uncomfortable hugging people, you may want to ask yourself why. But don't worry; you can learn how to hug someone. Talk to a friend or a loved one—surely that person will be willing to help!

Never Put Yourself Down, Even Jokingly

Do you often put yourself down? Please stop it now. ***Never*** put yourself down. Even avoid joking about yourself, especially when you do it to get "attention".

How could anyone take you seriously, let alone respect you, if you talk negatively about yourself? We know that the self-deprecating things people say about themselves are born from low self-esteem, and how harmful that can be.

Here are some of the self-destructive comments I've heard people say on many different occasions:

- ***"Being the idiot that I am..."***
- ***"I am absolutely useless."***
- ***"Because I am always so stupid..."***
- ***"Silly me..."***
- ***"I am rubbish at..."***

Do you recognise yourself in these? You are, in essence, a soul. You were born from the God Source, and you were brave enough to come down here on this planet to experience life for the evolvement of your soul. That's a tremendous duty and you should feel extremely proud about that. Don't diminish your soul by saying silly things about yourself you know don't make any sense. I am not saying you have to be serious about yourself all the time; what I am talking about is constant negative self-talk, which is extremely harmful. By only talking of yourself in favourable terms you will command the respect, not only from others, but more importantly from yourself.

If you are brave enough to incarnate here and ride the roller coaster that is life, why would you ever feel the need to put yourself down? It's a spiritual slap in the face of your own soul!

If you don't want to be the victim,
stop being the victim!

Be Gentle With Yourself

Today I want you to make a list of good things about yourself below or in your journal. Aim for at least 10 things. If you struggle, ask your closest friends for help. What do they particularly like about you?

Your list could look like this:

- ***"I am great with kids."***
- ***"I am friendly."***
- ***"I am tidy."***
- ***"I am a good swimmer."***
- ***"I always seem to make other people smile."***
- ***"I am good at playing football."***
- ***"I care about my health."***
- ***"I am good at singing."***
- ***"I am organised."***
- ***"I am a good listener."***

Exercise: List 10 things you really like about yourself:

1. ______________________________
2. ______________________________
3. ______________________________
4. ______________________________
5. ______________________________
6. ______________________________
7. ______________________________
8. ______________________________
9. ______________________________
10. ______________________________

Now add 10 more things to your list!

1. ______________________________
2. ______________________________
3. ______________________________
4. ______________________________
5. ______________________________
6. ______________________________
7. ______________________________
8. ______________________________
9. ______________________________
10. ______________________________

Once you have made your list, sit back and reflect on these things you are good at. Read it over and over again. Notice how good it feels.... And no, you are not kidding yourself— everything you wrote on your list is true for you.

You must love and care for yourself, because that's when the best comes out.

Tina Turner

Do at Least One Nice Thing for Yourself Every Day

One habit I swear by is doing at least one nice thing for myself every day. Most of the time, we find ourselves doing a million and one things for ***someone else.***

I will forever remember the day my manager called me over in her office. She knew I was very busy outside of my daytime job with all my coaching studies and related projects. She also knew that I was one who always wants to deliver perfect work. However, I was trying to keep too many plates spinning at once. My manager (and I still think she's the world's best life coach) confronted me with an uncomfortable truth: that I was not going to be to able to keep all my plates spinning without making sure that I kept myself going first. I guess that was the moment I realised that effective coaching is not necessarily a walk in the park. Yes, it was time to face it: I was going to have to do something to restore balance in my overloaded schedule. I argued that it was good to be busy and that one day I would reap the benefits from working like mad. Again, she was the perfect coach by holding up a figurative mirror and saying, "Just how do you expect clients to benefit from working with you if you're simply too tired to help them properly?"

"Good God!" I thought. "You are supposed to support me as my manager." What I realised later is that she'd presented me with yet another example of her innate coaching skills. And she was right. The obvious answer to her question made me see that I wasn't going to be of much use as a personal coach if I'd be mentally exhausted all the time. She then told me a simple tip that I'll share with you here: to make a point of doing at least one nice thing for myself every day. She wouldn't allow me to do something related to my coaching assignments; it had to be something else. And that's when I chose to "make myself" sit down for a little bit every evening to reflect on my day and to re-energise.

Soon I started experiencing the tremendous benefits of doing this simple but important practice. I went from "making myself" to "allowing myself" to sit down and relax. Other ideas for creating more time for myself and restoring balance began to appear soon afterwards. And now I teach other people how they too can seriously improve the quality of their life by applying these tips.

Respect yourself enough to allow yourself to do something you really enjoy, every single day. It will become a positive addiction. Your "you time" doesn't have to take long, it doesn't have to be expensive, and it needn't take a great effort.

Here are some ideas:

- Sit down for a while and listen to your favourite piece of music
- Write a list of 10 things you are good at, just to remind yourself
- Go for a walk or bike ride
- Think about how you can make a difference today
- Praise yourself
- Treat yourself to something nice
- Watch something uplifting
- Meditate
- Call or write to a friend or family member
- Exercise
- Spend some time on your hobby
- Take a dog (yours or someone else's) for a walk
- Learn about something new

- Write in your diary
- Read a few chapters of a novel
- Feed the ducks
- Reflect on your day and notice what you did really well

Anything goes, as long as it makes you happy and gets you "spiritually involved". Watching any random programme on television is not what I'm referring to here. What I mean is to consciously spend some time every day doing something positive and uplifting for yourself. This will help you restore your work-life balance in a self-loving and constructive way.

You will be surprised at what a difference this habit will make to your life. Doing just one thing for the most important person in your life—***you!***—will help you to fully respect yourself, understand yourself better, stay happy, feel lighter, boost your health and so much more!

Question to ask yourself: What will I enjoy doing every day that will contribute to the growth of my soul?

Commune With Nature

The outside world is a wonderful place if we'd only look up from our desks or get out of the house to explore it! Simply by going outside, walking the dog, feeding the ducks, visiting the local park, strolling on a coastal path or even heading for the hills, you can make a positive impact on your life.

Being close to trees can be very beneficial to our health. Trees contain vast amounts of ***life-force*** energy. This is the **non-physical energy** that animates all living things on our planet. You and I have life-force energy in us. However, sometimes we may feel a little depleted, and spending time near trees to absorb an extra dose of this energy can be a wonderful boost to our soul. Whether you go for a picnic outdoors, sit beneath a tree to read a book or meditate, or even hug a tree, these are all wonderful ways to reconnect with nature in a very special way.

Hugging a tree is also the name of an exercise in qigong, also spelled "chi-gong" (the ancient Chinese art involving meditation, controlled breathing and movement). With this exercise, you stand with your feet open, grounded in the earth like the roots of a tree, your arms open wide as if embracing a tree, descending and spreading and drawing life-force energy upward into your body, mind and spirit. With all qigong exercises, we are able to receive light from the heavens while being grounded in the earth, achieving balance. As we breathe in and out slowly and deeply, we can imagine taking in positive healing white light and releasing our worries.

Green is the colour of healing and strength. By spending time communing with nature you will absorb its healing energies and feel stronger and more balanced. Trees are living things, so treat them with respect. Always silently "ask" the tree for permission to touch or hug it, and remember to express your gratitude when you leave the tree.

I find trees very inspirational in so many ways. It's extraordinary how one small seed can grow to become such a large masterpiece of nature. Trees are strong and powerful; they convert carbon dioxide into oxygen. Trees are the lungs of our beautiful planet. They survive the seasons and return to grow stronger and taller every year—they are a great source of inspiration for us all.

In all things of nature there is something of the marvellous.

Aristotle

Get involved in Holistic Healing

We all have innate healing powers. You do too. Your power to heal yourself and other people is an integral part of your soul's "package". Some people are more gifted at this, but with practice, anyone can develop their God-given healing skills.

Holistic healing aims to make a person "whole" again. A good balance between mind, body and spirit is vital to living a healthy and fulfilling life. Our pains and discomforts are merely symptoms of an imbalance. Rather than focusing on a particular physical ailment alone, the holistic therapist will concentrate on bringing balance back into the client's life. A good therapist is able to "kick-start" the body and mind's own healing processes.

Your healing skills can be varied: You could be a hands-on healer or emotions healer, or even both.

Hands-on types of healing and holistic therapies include:

- Energy-based therapies such as Reiki and chakra balancing
- Aromatherapy
- Acupuncture
- Reflexology
- Hot stone therapy
- Crystal therapy
- Qigong

Examples of holistic medicines (also known as alternative or complementary medicine):

- Acupuncture
- Traditional Chinese medicine
- Homeopathy

Examples of healing on an emotional level include:

- Counselling
- Life coaching
- Anxiety management

Benefits of joining a class in holistic healing:

- You can explore your innate talents
- You get to spend time with like-minded people
- You can make new friends
- You can network
- You might love it so much you want to start your own healing practice
- And most importantly, you can heal people!

Have people ever told you they feel better in some way after spending time with you? This is the best indicator that you are a healer. If you want to explore this further, search for a local class in holistic healing. These classes provide a safe and supportive environment to develop your healing skills. Exploring and developing your holistic healing skills is a wonderful way to grow spiritually and your soul will adore you for it.

You don't need to be a certified holistic therapist, doctor or nurse in order to heal someone. You can be a healer by simply offering someone a listening ear. Often simply being there is already an incredible support for someone who is in need of emotional or physical healing.

A healer plays the role of a catalyst and is someone who facilitates healing. No-one heals anyone else; it is the Universe that does the healing in the end, not the healer.

So how can I become a healer without the qualifications?

By making a conscious decision to be a healer. You can literally flick your healer switch on or off at any time. If you intuitively feel that somebody would really benefit from your energy and your presence, it's a sign for you to switch on your healing powers.

Anyone can be a healer. Some people may access it more easily than others, but everyone can develop this natural ability. This ability, however, will be different from person to person. Some may be more talented to heal physical ailments, some with emotional issues, while others may help people with spiritual growth, which plays a part in their healing.

Again, you don't need to perform miracles, simply spend a little bit of time offering a listening ear and some support, guidance or coaching.

Try a Holistic Therapy

You go to the doctor or dentist for checkups or when you are feeling sick. Of course, these visits are vital and necessary routines as part of a healthy lifestyle. How about trying something really different that can help you feel better overall, and not just physically, something that is so wonderful and revitalising it can heal you from the inside out? I guarantee you that, unlike the ones to the doctors, you will ***love*** your visits to your ***holistic*** practitioner.

The benefits of having holistic therapies can be nothing short of extraordinary as they focus on restoring balance between mind, body and soul, helping you to feel ***whole*** again. The healing received from these treatments takes place on physical, emotional, mental and spiritual levels.

Holistic therapies use non-invasive and non-pharmaceutical techniques and are often called ***complementary*** therapies because they can be used in addition to mainstream medicine.

Your holistic practitioner will focus on:

- Calming the nervous system
- Balancing hormones
- Stimulating circulation (though touching is not required)
- Dissolving energy blocks
- Facilitating inner calm

Holistic therapies stimulate your body to heal itself. By that, I mean that the body's own healing properties will be reactivated. But it goes much further than that, because in holistic therapies we believe health issues are not always caused by physical ailments.

Holistic treatments will support your spiritual growth because they deal with the ***underlying*** problem of the physical symptoms. If this problem keeps being ignored, it is unlikely that the symptoms will disappear or improve. Our spiritual growth is accelerated when we learn how to face mental and emotional issues and then confront them. Holistic therapies can give you the courage and motivation to explore these issues deeper. By doing this, you invite emotional and spiritual healing to take place, which will in turn promote the healing of your physical ailments.

As with all therapies please always take advice from your doctor before accepting any alternative medicine to your current treatment, and always follow your prescriptions.

Being a Reiki "Master" myself, which means that I have acquired an advanced understanding of Reiki and I am qualified to teach others, I would like to take this opportunity to expand more on this particular holistic therapy. Reiki is the Japanese word for ***Universal / Spiritual Life Force Energy***. Reiki Healing is using this energy as a complementary therapy that transcends cultural, political and religious boundaries. It complements and enhances all types of medical treatment and it can also act as path to personal and spiritual growth.

Reiki practitioners receive both thorough training in this ancient healing art and Reiki "attunements" which raise and accelerate their energy flow. The practitioner provides a Reiki treatment by the gentle act of "laying on of hands" with the ***intention*** to be of assistance. During a Reiki session, the person being treated is not "healed" by the practitioner. The person's healing comes from the life force flowing ***through*** the Reiki practitioner.

Reiki:

- Calms, relaxes and reduces stress
- Improves sleep
- Helps maintain/raise your energy level
- Can alleviate symptoms, e.g., of cramps, colds, headaches, sore throat etc
- Improves immune system
- Complements other healing modalities
- Accelerates physical healing

Reiki can be performed on a client while he is lying down, sitting or standing. Client and practitioner remain fully clothed at all times. There are no side effects or contraindications with Reiki; it is non-intrusive and safe for all ages. The Reiki practitioner will place his hands gently on top of your clothing over key positions on your body. A 1-hour Reiki treatment is the physiological equivalent of 3-4 hours sleep, making it one of the most advanced, natural stress reduction therapies available!

A great thing about receiving a Reiki treatment is that it often kick-starts important and much-needed changes in a person's life. Reiki Energy always "knows where to go", which means that when I am "channelling" Reiki the energy may benefit a client's physical body, but it can also work on mental and emotional blockages, and often it will work on both. I was recently asked to do an "emergency" Reiki session on someone who was suffering from severe depression due to being long-term unemployed. My client's dream was to pursue a career in the airline industry. After our Reiki treatment he was visibly more alert and radiant. He was excited about how peaceful and safe he had felt during the session and that he felt inspired to start looking for the perfect job again. A few days later his wife told me he had been invited for an interview at the local airport and that he was over the moon. Another week later he was offered the job!

The Myth of Inner Beauty

Many people believe that spirituality is only about inner beauty. That's a myth. It is very important to respect your body as well, for it is a part of your soul. All too often, the mind and body are looked at as separate things. But your body is ***not*** the temple of your soul. It is, together with your mind, an expression of your soul.

Your soul incarnates on this planet to grow. It takes on a human form to experience life as a human being. This means your soul has both a mind and a body. So why only take care of your mind?

Honouring your body is an extension of honouring life**.** Your body is the vehicle through which you experience life. It's important to keep that vehicle healthy and strong by eating nourishing food and doing exercise that is right for you. Consult with your doctor or gym staff to find out which type of exercise will give you the best results. A healthy body and a healthy mind work hand in hand; without one, you'll never be fully complete in the other.

Staying active can open your mind by allowing you to get out there and see what's going on around you. By interacting with society and walking around the park for example, you become a part of nature again and see the beauty of life for yourself rather than watching it on TV. Some people have the best ideas and bolts of inspiration while walking through the forest or just around the park feeding the ducks.

These moments can allow you to let go of the day-to-day stresses and get the oxygen and blood pumping around your body and into your brain, boosting your sense of wellbeing.

The importance of eating healthily is something most of us are thankfully aware of. Taking good care of our bodies is essential; if we don't then who else will? Usually just taking some small steps is all that's needed to get us on the right track. Cutting down on unrefined foods such as white bread, pastries, biscuits and cakes, and eating more fresh fruit and vegetables can make a huge difference to your wellbeing.

You don't have to cut everything out, but just cut down and replace the bad foods with alternative "good" ones. Depression, illness, fatigue, mood swings, headaches, lack of motivation and low self-esteem are just a few things that are caused by an unhealthy diet. Your body needs good food to work well. It's like putting diesel in a petrol engine car; it just won't work the same, and eventually it will give up!

People often ask me if I can help them overcome their addiction. First of all, depending on the nature of the addiction, I always recommend that you consult with a doctor first. Unless medically qualified, life coaches are not allowed to deal with medical issues and thus not allowed to diagnose. What usually does happen, however, during a coaching session is that the client will discover the underlying cause of the addiction, which can be deeply rooted. Issues like low self-esteem and insecurity can be addressed and worked on. When I help clients who are addicted to chocolate or nail biting, for example, I usually dedicate a lot of time focussing on boosting their levels of self-love and self-confidence.

The biggest breakthrough moment comes when they realise how good their situation will be once they leave the addiction behind them. During a coaching session, we paint a picture of the lighter life that awaits them. We then learn how to use positive affirmations to create healthy thoughts that will dramatically increase self-confidence and self-respect.

Keep Fit

Inner and outer wellbeing go hand in hand. Exercising helps to increase your flexibility and will stimulate the flow of oxygen, thus helping you to think more clearly. We all know how sometimes we feel a little stuck or overwhelmed, but when we go for a short walk or a run, we quickly feel better and often have new ideas and inspiration. As an added benefit, keeping fit will also reduce your chances of injury.

Try to make room for some basic exercise in your schedule; you will find it very helpful.

Question to ask yourself: How would I benefit from exercising more often?

Every form of exercise, no matter how basic, contributes to a healthy mind and a healthy body.

If you feel you need some help with this, I suggest you approach your local health club where qualified staff will be available to guide you in the right direction. They can even help you to find like-minded people who you can exercise with. This is also a fun way of meeting new friends!

A few benefits of regular exercise and keeping fit:

- Working out is a great way to help relieve stress and anxiety
- Exercise can reduce your risk of heart disease and stroke
- You will be more self-confident and have more energy
- Exercise uses up extra calories to help control your weight
- Keeping fit can help to reduce some of the effects of aging
- You will look better physically
- You will naturally sleep better

Imagine Your "Wings" Growing Stronger as You Get Ready for Your Day

This is a powerful exercise. It only takes five seconds and will give you a beautiful feeling instantly. Before you get dressed in the morning, raise your arms sideways and imagine them as being your wings. Now feel them extend, growing strong and beautiful.

Large and strong wings will:

- Protect you
- Support you during your day
- Reflect your self-worth
- Help you feel confident
- Make you more visible and attractive to others

Now get dressed and off you go!

Visualise Your Aura Reaching Out to People

Did you know that you can positively influence people with your aura? You can reassure, support, love and motivate someone without saying a word.

Your aura is a concrete, existing energy field that surrounds you and all living things. It consists of subtle colour radiances that surround your body. Each colour signifies a certain vibration that relates to psychical, mental, emotional and spiritual states.

The aura is very real and can be photographed using special equipment.

Here's an exercise you can try the next time you wish to reach out to someone but you can't find the right words: Imagine your aura expanding beautifully. You can fill it with your favourite colours or a bright white light. Add positive feelings and loving thoughts to it. Now imagine your aura touching the other person's aura. Remember, other people might not even know they have an aura around them. Very quickly they will become aware of some energy movement around them.

The person's higher self will usually allow your aura to merge with theirs. All the goodness that you have sent through your aura will be absorbed by the person you are trying to help.

As always, be creative with this. Here are some ideas:

Expand your aura towards other people when you:

- Feel they are in need of support
- Sense they need reassurance
- Want to let them know silently that you care
- Wish to send them love but you feel shy
- Want to attract people you like to yourself

There are no limits to this, but remember: Only expand your aura and reach out to others when you do it for the right reasons. You make a spiritual mistake if you try to send out negative vibrations to someone which will find its way back to you sooner or later. Keep in mind that it is the higher self of the person you want to reach who will decide whether or not your aura and positive vibrations will be allowed in. Don't force anything to happen. If it is meant to be, it will be accepted and welcomed.

Slow Down When Talking

A quick way to make a positive, composed and spiritual impact on people is to talk more slowly. We live in a fast-paced society and communication is often rushed. If you want to come across as confident and in control, you'll have to do something different: Talk slower.

If you wish to communicate effectively, you have to make sure you are ***understood***. It's easier than you think: Before you speak, wait for a few seconds to get clear on what you want to say. Ever had that annoying feeling of "Why did I say that?" If so, you probably spoke before thinking the message through.

Notice the "gap-filler" words in your speech. Words such as ***obviously, basically, actually, yeah, you know*** and so forth, and sounds like ***uh*** or ***errr*** dilute our message and are completely unnecessary. It is okay to use them occasionally, but some people overuse these gap fillers and make it harder for people to understand what they are talking about.

We use filler words for various reasons:

- We are not sure of what we are saying
- We talk too fast
- We are not self-confident
- We want to buy time
- It is a habit

What are ***your*** gap-filler words and sounds? Is there any particular word you tend to overuse? Reduce the number of gap fillers in your speech and your message will be clearer.

How to do this:

- ***Slow down*** when you speak
- Replace the gap filler with a short pause (hear it in your head, but don't say it)

By speaking fewer words, you'll be understood better. People will see you as a calm and relaxed person who's in control. This is sure to boost your self-confidence.

Sit Quietly for Two Minutes Every Day

Many people ask me how they can get more guidance from the Universe, their higher self, or their spiritual helpers, such as spirit guides, loved ones who have passed on or angels. You don't need to be a psychic medium or guru to receive valuable information to help you with your life. Some people think they never receive any messages or help. However, we all do, all the time. But how can you hear the messages when you don't listen?

Our busy lifestyles sometimes make it impossible for help to reach us. That's why so many people receive guidance when they are asleep, when the conscious mind is switched off.

Allow yourself to sit down quietly for just two minutes every day. Make it a habit. You can do this anywhere; you don't need a sacred meditation place. Calm your mind, think loving thoughts and let your mind wander.... Give your soul a break, don't force anything to happen. Just sit quietly and allow any messages from Spirit or your higher self to come through. Soon you'll discover the enormous benefits of doing this.

When we stop pushing and start allowing, miracles occur.

Think Back to What You Wanted to Become When You Were a Child

Are you struggling to find direction in life? If you wonder about what you are good at or what your life purpose is, think back to what you enjoyed doing as a child. What did you want to be as an adult? This was before other people told you what you ought to do with your life. Very often, the key to discovering your life's dream can be found in your childhood.

Question to ask yourself: What did I want to become when I was a child?

When I was a child, I wanted to become an entertainer. I remember always enjoying dressing up, the drama, the attention I got from people whenever I was "performing" but most of all I remember my strong desire to entertain people so that they would feel better. Of course as I grew older I explored different options, but both my old job (airline crew member) and today's "job" as coach, trainer and lecturer turn out to be closely linked to my childhood dream job: entertainer. The cabin crew position was the "dressing-up" part, and today's position is the "entertaining" part. After all, isn't coaching people about finding creative ways to feel better in life?

Travel, Study and Expand Your Horizons

Accelerate your spiritual growth by ***nourishing your soul.*** You may have many learning opportunities in life by staying inside your comfort zone, but often the real juice is to be found elsewhere. Would you like to visit interesting places? Do you want to learn new skills? Are you ready to move on in life? Travelling and studying are fantastic ways to further yourself spiritually.

Don't let anyone hold you back when you feel ready to go on a journey. I have travelled on my own, and it was on those trips that I met some of the most amazing and inspiring people. Some people fear that travelling alone will be difficult and dangerous. They think they will be lonely, but it's quite the opposite. You don't have to leave everything behind and hitchhike to the other end of the world, you know. If you like the idea of travelling alone but you are a little unsure, try looking for a weekend seminar or a workshop nearby that appeals to you. You are bound to meet like-minded people and learn something new as well. If you like the experience, you may wish to explore longer trips and going further away.

Studying to expand your mind does not always mean sweating over university courses. Whether you want to do a long or short course there are many fantastic options open to you, from home study, tele-classes or even private tuition. By searching online, visiting your local library or community centre, you will open yourself up to the vast array of options available to you.

The easiest way to expand your mind is by doing things that bring you ***joy***. Why don't you treat yourself to a well-deserved holiday or an interesting training course?

Here are some ideas to help you get a sense of what's out there:

- Counselling and stress management
- Sports and fitness
- Animal healing
- Cookery classes
- Anatomy and physiology
- Speech and language skills
- Business and management
- Childcare and education
- Creative writing
- Yoga therapy
- Photography
- Art or life drawing
- Beauty therapies
- Psychology
- Complementary therapies
- Healthcare
- Holistic image consulting
- Egyptology
- Life coaching and life skills
- Continuing professional development
- Writing, editing and publishing skills
- Psychic healing
- Criminology
- Philosophy

Express your creativity in ways that feel good to *you*.

Are you creative? Do you allow yourself to express yourself in creative ways?

Here are some ideas:

- Paint
- Design a website
- Act
- Cook (get creative in the kitchen)
- Write (an article, a book, a play, a piece of music…)
- Host your own Internet radio show
- Create your own videos
- Organise a talk about your favourite topic

Being creative with your talents and skills is the lifeblood of your soul. It longs to express itself.

Have you ever enjoyed doing something so much it seemed to consume you? Maybe you experienced this when you were making a drawing or writing a poem. This process is called ***channelling:*** allowing your subconscious mind and higher self to flow "through" you.

Everybody channels from time to time. Have you ever said something and then thought, "Where did that come from?" or "I don't know why I said that!" Those are examples of channelling.

Calm Your Mind

If you suffer from feeling overwhelmed caused by an overactive mind, I suggest you yell silently in your head, ***"Stop!"*** to the thoughts racing through your head. When you do this, you can take a step back, acknowledge what's happening and regain order and composure. Have you been worrying too much? Have you overloaded yourself with negative thoughts?

Excessive worrying stunts our spiritual growth.

A loud ***"Stop!"*** in your head can bring instant relief. Take a few deep breaths, think some positive affirmations, such as "All is well and I am safe" and you will quickly feel lighter again. Notice how calming your mind and slowing down did not stop the world from turning. There are many additional methods to help you to calm your mind such as yoga, breathing exercises, meditation or even visualisation. Choose whichever method resonates with you. If you are a big caffeine drinker you may also want to cut down on your consumption, as an excess can sometimes lead to a racing mind.

Avoid Watching or Listening to the News

It's important to be kept informed about what goes on in the world, but it can be detrimental to your emotional wellbeing when you expose yourself too much to negative news. And unfortunately that's precisely what the news channels offer us.

It's a constant update on:

- Disasters
- Financial crises
- Death
- War
- Abuse
- Failure
- Loss

My coaching clients report a dramatic positive change to the start of their day when they reduce their intake of bad news. They now only listen to the headlines or quickly scan through them on their Internet homepage, but after that, they play uplifting music or audio books or enjoy peaceful silence.

This is a perfect example of how small changes can really improve the quality of your day.

When you stop allowing the media to feed your conscious and unconscious mind (because the news is everywhere) with bad and depressing messages, a lighter way of being can emerge.

Use Sticky Notes With Positive Statements to Quickly Change the Way You Think and Feel

I ***love*** this one!

Think about it: Everywhere around you, there are things that can make you feel worried or upset:

- Bills on the kitchen table
- Credit card statements on your desk
- Reminder letters about insurances that are about to expire
- A huge shopping list on the fridge door
- A picture in your wallet of an ex-partner you can't let go of
- The TV news channel full of sad news playing in the background
- And ***many*** more

It is almost as if we surround ourselves with negativity at times. So if you are ready to feel lighter and happier more often, here's a very useful tip: Give yourself something ***positive*** to see or hear. And these are some ways you can start right now: Get some bright-coloured Post-it sticky notes and think carefully about what you would like to be "told" or "reminded of". Write this down on your sticky notes and put them in visible places. The more you see the messages, the more you will resonate with them. They are those loving statements of truth you crave so much but are hard to find. So why not create them yourself? They are guaranteed to lift your spirits and make you feel great.

If you are worried about others seeing your sticky notes, keep them in places where only you can see them: inside your wallet, bathroom cupboard or nightstand drawer. Or stick one on your bookmark or in your car—the possibilities are only limited by your imagination!

Here are some great examples of positive affirmations that my clients use on their sticky notes:

- ***"All is well and you are loved."*** (Imagine reading ***that*** first thing in the morning)
- ***"You are protected and safe."*** (A nice one for when you get in your car, pay your rent, go to sleep at night and wake up in the morning)
- ***"Hello, you beautiful soul."*** (Something we all like to hear)
- ***"You are an inspiration for others."*** (That will stimulate you to reach your goals)
- ***"You are a really a great parent."*** (For when you're feeling doubtful)
- ***"You are doing really well."*** (In times of uncertainty)

Sing!

Singing is a great way to feel lighter quickly and for generating that much desired feel-good factor, and it's good for your health too!

You don't need to sing an entire opera to experience the benefits. Try singing on your way to work, in the shower, with the kids, in the garden, in the park or anywhere you feel like it. Your soul will love you for it! It's like a welcome break from all the stress and worry of your daily life.

Research tells us that singing promotes both a healthy heart and an enhanced mental state. Singing is like a workout for your upper body; it's an aerobic activity that can improve the efficiency of your cardiovascular system and stimulate you to take more oxygen into your bloodstream, leading to increased alertness.

Some of the most important benefits of singing:

- It's an energetic and euphoric mood-lifter
- It helps you increase your personal confidence and overcome shyness (great for public speaking, public appearances, job interviews, and so forth)
- Singing helps reduce the feelings of depression or anxiety through the release of endorphins
- It helps with lung development and strengthening
- Singing sends oxygen to the blood system and brain (increased concentration and alertness)

Make More Time for Yourself

If you "live" for the weekend,
you are sure to "die" five days out of seven!

What do you like to do, and how can you do more of it? This is a coaching question that I use when clients are stuck in the rut they have created for themselves.

Interestingly, rather than answering the question, they immediately come up with reasons why it is *not* possible for them:

- ***"What I really like to do is not good enough."***
- ***"It's not a real job."***
- ***"It will never make me enough money."***
- ***"I should stop dreaming about it."***

And, of course:

- ***"I don't have the time to do it."***

Strangely enough, most people do find the time to watch virtually any TV programme or to spend hours on the Internet, and not necessarily in a productive way!

Does this ring a bell? If so, I encourage you to take a good look at your day/week/weekend, and see where you could create more time for yourself.

Once you take some small steps you will realise it is possible to create more time for yourself. You can use this time in a way that will benefit your personal growth and the growth of your soul, indulging in what you want to do, not what your family or society expect you to do.

Use it as an opportunity to connect to your inner light, your passions and your desires.

Exercise

Take five minutes now and below, or in your journal, note down the structure of a typical day in bullet points, and include ***everything.***

Example:

Wednesday

- Shower and getting ready
- Breakfast
- Driving to work
- Work and morning break
- Lunch
- Work and afternoon break
- Driving home after work
- Stopping off at the supermarket
- Relaxing and going through your post
- Cooking
- Relaxing and watching TV
- Spending time on the phone with friends
- Surfing the Internet
- Bedtime

My day: ....

Now take a moment to reflect on where and how you could use your time more efficiently:

Are there things you could do differently?

What could save you some valuable time?

What could you leave out?

Where can you prioritise?

Here are some practical examples of ideas that my clients and I have come up with together during coaching sessions on time management:

- "Rather than listening to the radio on my way to work, I now listen to audio books. It's very exciting, and I save valuable time by not having to sit down and read the book at home."
- "I used to sit and watch just about any TV show. Now I go to the gym where they have TV screens, get to watch my favourite show, and have a great workout too!"
- "I go out for a short walk now instead of staying in the office at lunchtime. It feels great to get some fresh air and exercise. I return to the office feeling revived and ready for my afternoon."
- "I didn't realise I was wasting so much valuable time by driving to the supermarket after work every day. I now do a weekly shopping on Friday evening. By doing this, I add at least 20 "extra" minutes to my day. This is the time I believed I didn't have to do my meditations. Thank you so much!"

Every moment lived fully is a moment of transcendent alchemy, of fire transforming dull metals to dazzling gold.

Anonymous

Buy Yourself Flowers

You buy flowers for those you love and appreciate. You even add a little card with a lovely greeting on it. When you give the flowers to that special person, you see their face light up. As you learn to love and appreciate yourself more from what you have been reading in this book, I would like you to buy some nice flowers for ***yourself***. It doesn't matter if you're male or female; everybody likes their living room or office to look nice, and flowers, or an interesting looking plant, can make a positive difference. You can even write a little card to yourself. Why not? "Thank you for being you" or "Well done on your achievements" and think how good it will feel to read that message and remind yourself of how great and deserving you really are. Simply leave out your name and no-one will know that you bought the flowers for yourself.

Be Open to Love

Finding love is one of the great missions in life. Or is it? Love brings us both joy and pain. It has inspired the world's greatest creative talents and is a billion-dollar business. It seems that in order to be happy and totally fulfilled in life, everybody ***must*** find love. Is it any wonder that not much good will come when the pressure is on like that?

In today's society you are almost deemed a failure if you don't find love. Surely there must be something wrong with you if you're turning 35 and still haven't found the love of your life. Or maybe you are just too difficult. Yeah, that's it; you are a difficult person—that's probably why people are not attracted to you.

We've all heard these kinds of ridiculous conclusions. They are destructive for two good reasons: They hurt you, and they affirm the absurd belief that finding your true love is an absolute requirement for a happy life.

Don't get me wrong; I know how great it is to be able to share precious time with a partner. But if that person hasn't crossed your path yet, don't worry too much about it. Love is energy, and it can be experienced in many other ways, too. Be excited about your career, do something nice with your friends, go on a holiday, join a gym and keep fit.... You can learn what love is by ***giving*** it to others first. You can ***be*** love. In fact, you are already pure love, because you are a part of the

God Scurce, and that ***is*** the very essence and energy of love.

Rather than demanding love, simply be ***open*** to love. "Love on demand" simply doesn't work. It may do for a few days, months, or even years, but real and unconditional love will only flow towards people who are open to receiving it. Love will reach people who have already connected to their inner light and who love themselves enough to avoid having to ***demand*** it from other people.

The door to the human heart can be opened only from the inside.

Spanish proverb

Explore Your Sexual Desires

Sex is important and physical intimacy is part of being human. From a spiritual point of view, we could say that in order to fully experience life in human form, your soul wants you to have sex to experience what it feels like. But there is more to it. Sex opens all your chakras (your body's energy centres) and your sexual desires are a vital part of your inner light. So if you want to connect to your inner light, you should also explore your sexual desires.

It is unfortunate that so many people suppress their sexual dreams. Please know that if it is a dream, it is a dream of your soul. And that's why we are here, to follow the dreams of our soul.

Blocked sexual energy can lead to:

- Frustration
- Depression
- Guilt
- Anger
- Violence
- Low self-confidence
- Illness

There are many spiritual teachers, coaches and support groups who can offer you the help and understanding you are looking for.

Exploring your sexual desires and working toward clearing any blocks ***you have created for yourself*** will greatly assist you on your path of personal and spiritual growth.

Are you ready to embrace this very important part of your life? Sex is meant to be a wonderful experience and it can truly be a "merging of souls". Most people spend so much time and energy trying to find "the one" very special person they are meant to be with. Now there are more than 6.5 billion people on our planet. "Good luck!" I say.

I am not advocating sleeping around with anyone you remotely like, but do you really want to wait until Mr. or Ms. Right comes along to experiment and discover what feels good to you? What guarantees that the partner of your dreams will share your sexual desires?

Live now. Honour yourself. Honour your dreams. Let go of guilt.

Some things are so simple if only we didn't complicate them.

Let Go of Friends and People Who Hurt You

As part of your spiritual growth, it is important to learn about being tolerant and understanding. However, when people continuously hurt you with deliberate intent, you will have to respect yourself enough to remove yourself away from them.

This may seem like a daunting task, but you will be so much better off without the arguments and emotional pain.

Why do these people hurt you?

- Are they envious of you?
- Do they not understand you?
- Do they have issues?
- Do they use you to vent their frustration?
- Are they bored?

It may be that you have simply outgrown certain friendships and relationships, and if so it's time to move on. Follow your heart, for it will always tell you the truth.

Sometimes we need to de-clutter our lives, and that includes leaving some friends and people. This is a natural process and takes place in order to create space to welcome new relationships into your life, people who you can truly connect with on a "soul" level.

When you allow this to happen, you will be overwhelmed by the love and friendship these people will have to offer you. You will see!

But what if I love the person who hurts me?

You can still love them. You can send them your love and blessing. But then take a step back and reflect on what the rest of your life will be like with that person in it, constantly hurting and degrading you (even though you "love" them).

Put on your spiritual tinted glasses, and look at the person who hurts you for the unique soul that he is. That soul is here to experience "hurting" other people and making someone's life miserable. Looking at the situation this way will help you put things into perspective. They have ***their*** learning opportunities in life. And so do ***you.*** Your lesson could be learning to draw a line under a bad situation and to move on.

You are a beautiful person. And you wouldn't be reading this if you weren't interested in creating a lighter life for yourself. Lay your burdens down. So the choice is yours: keeping the doors to your future firmly closed or grabbing the key ***now*** and unlocking them.

Reality check: Do you surround yourself with people who make you feel better or those who drain you?

Surround Yourself With White Light

As an extension to your aura, imagine a beautiful white light surrounding you. This light is a spiritual tool for protection. It comes directly from the Universe, God, your angels or whatever you wish to call it. What matters is that this light will shield you as you go about your day. It's especially helpful when you are in public spaces as often the energy in those places is heavy and may affect you. Have you ever walked into a room and felt uncomfortable or developed a headache from sitting in a shared office or waiting room? Chances are that you are sensitive to these energies, and when you pick up on them, they can certainly affect you and knock you off balance.

Surrounding yourself with white light is very helpful because it will:

- Give you an instant feeling of security
- Boost your confidence
- Make you feel and look more radiant
- Attract positive people and situations to you
- Keep negative people and situations away from you (the darkness can't stand the light)
- Protect you from germs and diseases

How to visualise being surrounded with white light:

- **Picture a light bulb *(a big one!) and place yourself in the centre, where you would normally find the wire filament.***
- ***Try it—you will be amazed at how effective this is.***

I was once at the gym when the fire alarm went off. I was in the middle of a workout and was covered in sweat when we were told to leave the building immediately. It was winter and ice-cold outside. Without a towel or jumper, I felt I would fall ill or at least get a cold. Knowing we would not be allowed to be back inside the building soon, I decided to call upon the white light of the Universe to protect me. Immediately, I felt safe, warmer and protected against the wind and rain. Even after spending more than 45 minutes outside, I didn't become ill or even catch a cold!

Be Authentic

As I mentioned earlier, there are more than 6.5 billion people on this planet.

Let me ask you two questions:

- When there are already so many 'others' why try and copy them?
- Wouldn't it be nice to find a way to stand out?

Being authentic in everything that you do is one of the keys to a healthy and balanced life. When you are authentic in your words and actions, you will truly live in alignment with your own values and beliefs. If you are a looking for a fast track to feeling lighter, consider being more authentic as you walk through life.

- Do you secretly dream of being accepted by people for who you really are without having to play a role?
- Are you happy in general, but do you wish to really start using your innate skills and talents?
- Do you long to pursue a dream and be genuinely successful in life?

Be more authentic, in everything you do. It will give you tremendous benefits.

Do you often find yourself saying "yes" in order to please people, to get their approval, or to avoid conflict? If so, challenge yourself to learning to say "no" the next time. If your heart is telling you "no" there's usually a good reason, and chances are you already know that reason. Learning to say "no" is an important part of your spiritual growth.

The more you say "yes" when you mean "no", the more you show to the Universe that you don't respect yourself enough yet.

I once heard somebody say, "The first hundred 'no's' are the hardest!"

That's true, you know. I am a person who enjoys giving to the world. So when I discovered that I could still be a ***good person*** without having to say "yes" all the time, it helped me tremendously!

Learn how to be "lovingly assertive" and authentic, and you will have people respecting you in no time.

How Being Authentic Brought me the Joy I Longed For

When I graduated as a certified coach from my coaching college, I was told that if I wanted to make real money from coaching and to be successful, I should focus on offering my services to wealthy people—people who have the disposable income but are not fulfilled in life.

I thought this through and could see the benefits of doing this, and I also had a good idea of where to find these clients. I created a standard life coaching website and was hopeful.

But in my heart, I knew that my real interest was to help people grow ***spiritually***. However, some people around me advised against setting up a spiritual coaching practice because they thought that the word ***spirituality*** would "scare" people.

And so I spent a few months waiting for those affluent and frustrated people who would benefit from the help I had to offer to show up.

But they didn't.

By now I had invested a huge amount of time, means, and energy in my coaching practice and I wasn't going to give up! I decided to connect to my ***inner light***. It was time to be ***authentic*** in my coaching work. Against all advice and feedback from people, I began to talk about what I really wanted to discuss: practical spirituality. I ***knew*** that many people would benefit from what I had to say and offer.

It was as if the spiritual floodgates had opened. Creative ideas, new concepts, opportunities, invitations for lectures, and above all, ***clients*** came my way.

And all this started happening because I was being truthful with myself. I locked on to my inside. I knew that if I was to become truly happy, I would have to follow my own path. Helping people feel lighter by showing how they too can become more authentic is one of the dreams of my soul. Connecting to my inner light allows me to live that dream.

When you look into the mirror, you see yourself.

When you look into the mirror of your Soul,
you'll see your Self.

And when you look into the mirror of your Self,

you'll see the path.

Only Help Those Who *Want* to be Helped

Something I had to learn the hard way was to stop wasting my energy trying to help people who were simply ***not ready*** to be helped.

Years ago I spent many sleepless nights worrying about how I could best support certain people; it used to totally consume my time and energy.

Being "someone who likes to help people" I used to think that it was my duty to do so. I would unconditionally give my time, money, ideas, love, patience, trust and support to those in need. Some, but not all, would benefit from my help and I used to feel somehow disappointed with myself when they didn't feel better after talking to me. I thought I had failed. But as my interest in spirituality and self-improvement began to grow, I discovered a very important spiritual principle: Only help those who ***want*** to be helped.

It is not good for you to help people who are not willing to receive what you offer. It is ***disrespectful*** towards your own soul. Instead, focus on using all that valuable time and energy to explore your own dreams and goals, and if you wish on helping others who ***are*** ready.

Trying to force your help onto someone is never a good idea. It stops the other person from taking responsibility for their behaviour and from learning their own lessons in life. If you are always trying to prevent someone from hitting rock bottom, you can make the process even more painful. This can be hard for most people to understand, but when I learned that concept for myself years ago, it really did help me—and, in turn, others.

Sometimes you need to ***allow*** someone to hit rock bottom, and give that person the ***opportunity*** to reassess their situation and options. It is probably one of the most exciting, yet challenging, spiritual acts of kindness you can ever make.

So, if you are now wondering when or when not to help someone, I would recommend that you ask them one simple question: "How willing are you to be helped?"

Remember, it's not because they approach you with a problem that they are ***willing*** to be helped, sometimes it is only to get some attention. There's a huge difference.

Question to ask yourself: Do I allow people to learn their own "lessons" in life?

Make sure that your happiness doesn't depend entirely upon making other people happy. This may sound strange coming from a life coach, but there's something valuable here that I want to make you aware of. Far too many people exhaust themselves trying to please others, at any time and at any cost. Depending on the approval of others will drain you sooner or later. Chances are you already depend on the approval of your managers at the office, so why put yourself under even more pressure outside of work? Many people go out of their way continuously in order to make other people happy. I am not saying that is a bad thing, but it will be detrimental if your entire self-esteem and confidence depend upon it.

Imagine, for example, if a motivational coach's happiness and self-image depended on "having to make everybody a more successful person". Can you see how unrealistic goals like that would soon make the coach feel like a failure? It simply is impossible to please everyone. First of all, not everybody is ready or willing to become successful, and, secondly, the coach can only experience ***real*** happiness and boost his self-worth when he was able to help those people who made a conscious decision to use the coach's services. That means those clients will be open to receiving the coach's support and will bring their own wisdom, creativity and intelligence to the coaching appointments.

Give because you want to give. Love because you want to love. Sponsor because you want to sponsor. Help because you want to help. Listen because you want to listen. Know and feel when enough is enough.

Question to ask yourself: Do I always want to help people only to make myself feel good?

Organise a Charity Event for Like-Minded Spiritual People

A fun way of giving back to society, while making new friends in the process, is by organising a charity event. Choose a topic that inspires you and that others will find helpful, and advise people that their donations will go to charity.

You can keep your costs very minimal, and the possibilities are endless:

- Any kind of demonstration
- Meditation evening
- Film screening
- Holistic healing workshop
- Group fitness activities such as a sponsored walk or fun run

There is great spiritual value in organising events for people. It is very well perceived by the Universe and accelerates your spiritual growth, for one of the quickest ways to achieve happiness is by making other people happy.

These are some benefits:

- You help people help themselves
- You can learn from the people who come to your event
- You make new spiritual friends
- You can give and receive networking opportunities

- People's feedback can help you feel fulfilled and loved
- You offer people a safe space for personal and spiritual development

What you'll need:

- A venue (this can be your own house or you can hire a room)
- To advertise your event (keep it cheap, use the Internet or word of mouth, put up an advertisement at work or in the library, and so forth)
- A topic you are passionate about (it will help you greatly to attract participants)
- An interesting event which will benefit attendees
- To be able to host the event yourself, or invite a guest speaker

If you are a spiritual person and your dream is to meet like-minded people and share your interests, organising your own charity events is the quickest and easiest way to achieve your goal. The joy you get from organising events for people and helping them grow spiritually is pure ecstasy for your soul. It will make you fly higher than any praise you'll ever get from your boss at work. The feedback I have received from the spiritual events I have hosted or presented at has been wonderful. People really do value activities such as these that are from the heart.

Reward Yourself Often

That's right, reward yourself often! Rewarding yourself, however, is not the same as spoiling yourself; let me explain. You can buy yourself nice things that will make you happy, but that feeling will only last for a short time. When you treat yourself to a chocolate bar, it may lift you, but only for a few minutes. Spoil yourself by buying a really expensive watch, and there's a good chance you'll be bored with it by next Christmas.

What I mean by rewarding yourself is not about spending money or chasing a quick emotional boost; it is much more constructive, it's about ***investing*** in you. When we reward ourselves we acknowledge the importance of the result of our actions and respect our hard work and commitment.

If living a successful life can be equated to constructing your temple, then rewarding yourself is the bricks and mortar that holds it all together. When you reward yourself, you erect meaningful support systems for yourself. Do you see how this is very different from simply spoiling yourself?

When I was doing my coaching studies, each time I passed an exam or finished an assignment successfully, I would reward myself by investing in a product that would in turn help me grow my coaching business. Rewarding yourself is an incredible way of staying motivated and giving yourself something valuable.

Review Your Values and Beliefs Have They Changed?

Everything changes. They say that change is the only constant in life. This is also true for your values and beliefs. As you grow older, your vision about your life and the world is bound to change, and rightly so. As more and more experiences come your way, your values and beliefs will undoubtedly be affected.

You change and grow as a person, and now is a good time to take a look at how some of your values and beliefs may no longer be serving you, and could, in fact, be hindering you from moving forward.

Example 1: You dream of travelling by yourself to some faraway destination but you always believed that such journeys should never be taken a one. Can you see how your belief is stopping you from living a more joyous life?

Example 2: You are in a relationship that is no longer satisfying your basic needs. You have invested a lot of time, love and energy into trying to make it work. In your heart you know it would be better for you to move on and find another partner who can give you what you need, but perhaps you value "security" and therefore you don't dare to explore your desires. By sticking with what you know, for the wrong reasons, can you see how you may be missing out on a more suitable partner?

Example 3: You are stuck in a job you loathe. You know the time is right to set up that business you've always dreamed of. You long to be a self-employed professional, and you want to make a good living. However, when you were a child, your father, who was self-employed, was no longer able to keep the business going and went bankrupt. Witnessing this traumatic experience as a child may have left you with the belief that running your own business is dangerous and will most likely result in failure. After all, your father was your hero and if he wasn't able to be successful in business, who would? A belief like this can be so powerful that it can hold you back from walking the career path that is right for ***you.***

So many people are stuck, yet they have dreams and goals, but their values and beliefs are so strongly rooted that they barricade the doors to the very change and opportunities they are longing for. You don't have to leave your comfort zone to do this; simply ***expand*** it. If you are too set in your ways, you may be missing out on the life you want. The following is an exercise to do in your journal or below to see if you may be missing out:

Exercise: Fill in the following statements:

"I wish to do____________________in my life, but it will be difficult because I believe that____________________________"

"I dream of being more________________________ but that will never happen because I believe that________________________"

Who would you be without these limiting beliefs? Now is a good time to let them go.

Contact a Spiritual Life Coach to Help You Connect to Your Inner Light and Develop Your Spiritual Side

Case Study: Mia Wants to Leave the Corporate World

Mia was intrigued by the line on my website that says, "Christoph connects his clients to their inner light". She contacted me and we scheduled an exploratory chat. It was during that initial conversation that Mia told me she was ready to connect to her "inner light" but she had no idea where or how to start.

Over the course of the next coaching sessions we explored together what she wanted to have more of in her life and what direction she wanted to go in. Mia was a busy woman with a family and a great career, yet she knew something was missing. In fact, it was already there. Mia wanted to become a holistic therapist, and she turned to me for coaching to bring it out.

Soon she went from being stuck and scared to discovering all the options that were right for her and, indeed, available to her. Her thinking and beliefs changed from "I can't" and "I shouldn't" to "I can!" and "Now is a perfect time to start!"

Within five weeks of our first appointment, Mia found a way out of the corporate world and is now the owner of a successful holistic practice. She is very busy but has discovered new ways of creating more quality time for herself and for her family.

It's good to have someone available to you on your life's journey, someone who understands you when others don't and who can really bring out the very best in you. This is exactly what life coaches do: They help you to create a more fulfilling and lighter life by connecting you to, as I like to call it, your inner light. No wonder coaching has received so much positive media attention over the past few years.

A spiritual life coach provides coaching sessions with a spiritual, non-religious approach to help you establish your dreams and goals, and identify the obstacles and strategies to overcome obstacles and lead a winning life. Together, you can collaborate to help you shape a life that's more balanced and fulfilling.

Through powerful, inspiring and comfortable coaching sessions, the coach and client will create a partnership to:

- Identify your goals (what do you really want from life?)
- Explore the obstacles to obtaining these goals
- Find solutions to the obstacles (solutions that are perfect for you!)

During the consultations, your coach:

- Offers a safe space to develop yourself spiritually
- Asks powerful, direct questions
- Genuinely appreciates and supports you
- Assists in setting goals, planning and strategising
- Gives perspectives, options and suggestions to create awareness and catalyse your own solutions

When you are working with a spiritual coach, you will:

- Accelerate your spiritual growth (learning and applying)
- Do more than you would do on your own
- Learn to feel whole, balanced and fulfilled
- Become the person you have always wanted to be

In each coaching session you choose the focus of conversation while the coach listens and offers observations and insights. Your coach will also ask powerful questions to help you clarify your situation and keep you focused. Through your conversations you will identify action steps to help you design the life of your dreams.

Knowledge is power; spirituality is fulfilment.

Case Study:
From "Trying" to "Doing!"

"I just wanted to thank you for waking me up so that I've finally started to have a positive attitude towards life. Of course, I have tried to approach life positively before, but I somehow always slipped back into old habits, probably because of my 'trying attitude'. Now I've finally stopped trying and started to **do** things and I can feel the difference. Thanks a lot, Chris."

Tatiana S. (Manchester, UK)

Exercise: Take a moment now to complete the following statement below or in your journal:

If only I had the right support, guidance and understanding, I would do/achieve:

But I can't do it yet because my biggest obstacles are:

The opportunities are there,
making the effort is rare.

Ask for Help—Don't Struggle Unnecessarily

Strong people ask for help; weak people ask for pity. It's okay to ask for help with the things you find hard to cope with. Strong and successful people are not afraid to ask for help and guidance on their way to achieving important goals. Yes, they have to put in the hard work, but they'll make sure to surround themselves with encouragement and people they can learn from. Just look at your favourite athlete, pop star or anyone you respect. They are at the top of their game because they spent countless hours working to reach perfection, and to do that, they asked for help.

I admire people who come to me for coaching. They wish to achieve their goals and realise that it will be an easier and more pleasant process if they can get help from someone who has trained extensively to help them with their requirements. This has nothing to do with being vulnerable, but everything to do with being strong and persistent. Coaching is for people who are ***serious*** about creating change in their lives and thus not afraid of confrontation with their own worst fears and challenges.

Are you good at asking for help? Or does the thought alone make you feel nervous? Would you benefit more, and be able to make your life more comfortable, if only you'd dare to ask for help? If so, what's stopping you? Do you have certain beliefs that hold you back? Or do you simply feel too proud to ask for support in life? Whatever the reason, if you are serious about going after your goals and following the dreams of your soul, you will want to have that extra guidance and help available to you. When I decided to write this book, I was so excited that at first I felt I could do it all by myself, without any assistance. Let me safely say that I was in for a surprise! Obviously, it was me who would have to write the book, but I had not the faintest idea about all the other aspects of getting a book out there!

I am a very independent guy but imagine where I would have been, if I'd been too stubborn to look for, and ask for, help. It was thanks to the expertise from professionals in the field of book designing and publishing that I was able to achieve the goal that I was so excited about.

Turn your face to the sun and the shadows fall behind you.

Maori proverb

Join Local and International Support Groups

Loneliness can cause fear, and fear is destructive. I don't mean feeling lonely occasionally if you are bored, but rather the feeling of "being different" that so many of us experience and that sets us apart in our minds from other people. One of my clients recently told me he feels lonely even when he's surrounded by his best friends. This can happen when "your group", the like-minded people who are able to give to you on the energetic level ***you*** need, is missing.

If this is the case for you at the moment I suggest you look at this as "waiting time". Know that they ***are*** coming, and trust that the Universe will send to you those souls with whom you'll be able to share your journey. A great way of giving the Universe the "green light" is by joining a local or international support group whose interests mirror your own.

There are many benefits:

- You have opportunities to connect with like-minded people
- You can get support and encouragement
- You could grow your business by networking
- You'll be able to share your experiences and ideas
- You have an opportunity to inspire others

Support groups are generally very affordable since many offer a free membership. The Internet or your local library is a great place to start looking for the right group for you; there are support groups for virtually any topic.

Question to ask yourself: How would I benefit from getting extra support on my journey?

Don't be afraid to seek help and support in life. Strong people ask for help, weak people find themselves suffering in a lonely corner. If you are ready to find new motivation and inspiration, the Universe ***will*** guide you to it.

When I first had the initial concept for my spiritual organisation, I felt I would need assistance to get the project off the ground. I started using the following affirmation every day: "I am grateful that the Universe brings to me the people with the rights skills, means and intentions to help me build my spiritual centre. One year later, I was surrounded by almost 100 people who inspired and helped me to develop my project.

Welcome Help from the Realm of Spirit

Help from whom? That's right: Spirit! You may be surprised at the title of this topic, and how it fits in a book about self-growth, so let me share with you why I decided to include it here.

Please rest assured that I am not going to tell you about ghosts. What I am going to share with you, however, is how richer my life became when I began to accept the help that Spirit was offering me. And when I say "Spirit" I am referring to the whole system of energies that reside on the spiritual plane. If you would ask me where that world of Spirit is, the best way I can answer that is by saying to you, "Everywhere".

Countless attempts have been made to understand where this "other world" is. In my opinion, it doesn't really matter where it is, but it would be helpful to keep an open mind about the real possibility that there is, indeed, a world of spirit that we cannot necessarily see. Many other books have been published about who lives there, what it looks like, what happens there, and so on, so I am not going to expand on that. What I will tell you about is the tremendous help that I have received from the spirit world in my life thus far; a kind of help that's so ***different*** from anything else, even thinking about it makes my heart glow. It's a resource that's always available to us and always ready to give. What we have to learn is how to ask the right questions.

We all have spirit guides, angels and other spiritual helpers. The help they offer us is unconditional; they never expect anything in return. The spirit world does, however, appreciate it when we humans make that extra bit of effort to make our lives more rewarding. Spiritual people always seem to be happier and more fulfilled and inspired, because they have a relationship with Spirit that gives them that extra boost of energy and motivation.

Whether you are going through a particularly challenging time in your life, or you are excited about reaching yet another goal, your spiritual helpers will be more than happy to assist. In fact, one of the reasons they are pleased about this is because by asking them for help, you acknowledge their very existence. Another important reason is that they grow considerably in their role as guide when they can reach out to you and help.

By the way, it's okay to ask for help. Don't be afraid that you are asking too much and that you may be "bothering" your spirit guides and other helpers. They have certain "rules" to follow, and they may therefore not be able to always help you immediately, but generally they quite happily oblige.

Make sure that when you ask for help, you are specific. Saying "Help me!" will be less likely to get you a detailed answer than when you say, for example, "Please help me find the perfect present for Steven, my best friend."

It is also important to note here that the world of Spirit operates on the law of non-interference so in order to get their valuable assistance in our life we have to ask for it. As always, be as specific as possible, and be careful what you wish for! Asking for something and then ending it with "this or something better for my highest good" acts as a kind of spiritual disclaimer when the universe has something even better in mind for us than we were asking for.

If you are not sure if "talking to spirits" is the way forward for you, simply replace the concept of "Spirit" with "The Universe" and let things flow. It's never a good idea to force things to happen. Like I said before, we are here to enjoy ***opportunities*** for the growth and evolution of our soul, which means that inevitably we will have to "learn lessons". If we always get the right help at the right time, we wouldn't learn half the lessons, and "graduation" would only take longer. That's why sometimes things "happen" to us and we feel abandoned, confused, lost and angry. Great! It's a wonderful opportunity to learn. Ever looked at the bad situations in your life that way? I believe it definitely makes things easier to understand. Generally speaking though, we ***do*** get a lot of help and support from "above" and it would be a shame not to see it by wearing our blindfolds of "narrow-mindedness".

"So, do you hear voices?" is a question I'm often asked. People who have developed the gift of ***clairaudience*** (the power or faculty of hearing something not present to the ear but regarded as having objective reality) can pick up sounds from the Universe and Spirit. When I ask for help and guidance, I don't hear voices but I do receive an answer that comes to me in a ***thought form***. I "feel" the answer in my mind. "And how do you know it's real?" is usually the next question I get. Because I ***trust*** it's real. What use is it to ask a question to Spirit, but when you get a reply think "Hmmm, wait a minute, what if it's not true?" What's the point in asking a question in the first place? And wouldn't you think you'd know the difference between your own thoughts and an idea that feels "different"? I do! There's a funny way in which my answers from Spirit are validated; if I receive the answer before I have finished asking the question, I know it's real. That's how it works for me.

Many people who have established a relationship with their spiritual helpers and the Universe, however, will receive help and answers in different ways. Some will ask a question, and when they turn on the TV or radio, they hear something that makes them realise aha!—that's what I needed to hear: There's the answer to my question. Or they will read something in a magazine at the doctors' or talk to someone in the queue at the checkout and receive an answer that way.

If you do decide to give asking questions to Spirit a try, I recommend you keep an open mind. You may quickly become aware of "something" but it may take months or years of practice. Simply trust it is working. "They" will always know the best way to reach out to you, so allow it to happen. Sometimes people are so excited about all this that they quite literally shut themselves off from receiving any communication at all because they force it too much to happen. So take your time, allow your mind to be still when you ask questions, and keep practicing.

I have been into spirituality since I was 11 years old. I have been blessed with a wonderful friend (she was a lady almost my mum's age) who introduced me to what she knew about the spirit world and the Universe, and she told me about my spirit guide. My life at that time was horrific at best, and I don't know if I would have made it without her. I remember being fascinated by everything she told me and especially how much everything resonated with me, but as the years passed, nothing really happened on the spirit front. My life continued to go downhill even further in the meantime, but I still didn't hear any voices or have visits from spirits in my bedroom at night (thank God because I probably wasn't quite ready for it!). But all the while I ***knew*** that the spirit world did exist and I trusted that feeling.

By the time I was 26 I had become a different person completely and was really enjoying life. I had become much more grounded and in tune with myself, and as a result, my energetic vibration really began to change as well. My aura was strong and large, and I became aware that my "connection" with the spirit world was beginning to grow rapidly. I realised that now was simply a better time for them to reach out to me. I was being protected and watched over when I was going through the rough years of my life, but it would have been very hard for Spirit to establish any direct communication with me; my mind was literally too preoccupied with sadness and darkness.

I am really pleased (and proud) that, despite the turbulent years, I have always trusted in my heart. I knew that we are not alone and that there is, indeed, a collective of higher forces out there with which we can connect. I still don't hear any voices but the thought forms and ideas are becoming clearer and more reliable every day. It's truly wonderful to have this relationship with Spirit and to trust it enough to allow it to guide me on my path, and all the while have complete freedom to do with my life what I want. We all have free will and Spirit will help and guide us when specifically asked, and sometimes even when we haven't! So begin asking for ideas, motivation, means and inspiration from your spiritual helpers and the Universe. They ***are*** available in the wings, eagerly awaiting your call.

Laughing is Good for You

Few things can make you happier faster than a good laugh, so it's a good idea to make sure there's plenty of fun stuff in your life to laugh about. Here's why laughing makes us feel so much better: It stimulates the release of endorphins in the brain. Endorphins are our body's natural feel-good chemicals, which promote an overall sense of wellbeing. A good laugh is also beneficial for your health: It will boost your immune system, decrease your stress hormones and increase immune cells and infection-fighting antibodies, thus improving your resistance to disease.

Physical, mental and social benefits of laughter:

- Laughter relaxes your muscles for up to 45 minutes
- It helps to relieve stress
- Laughter makes you shine more and thus be more attractive
- It decreases pain
- It helps to avoid conflict
- Laughter improves your mood quickly
- It supports a healthy heart (laughter improves the function of blood vessels and increases blood flow)
- It can enhance and strengthen relationships

Make time to watch a good comedy film, listen to a funny radio show, or spend some time with people who make you laugh (these are not necessarily your best friends!). I often watch a five-minute video clip on my laptop in the morning. After my breakfast and before I begin my work that I love so much, I will watch a clip on the Internet with bloopers, gags, or anything that makes me laugh. It's absolutely addictive. Laughing is so powerful it can shift emotions instantly. It will help you better cope with any stress and will, quite simply, make you feel good. What a great way to start your day! The choice is yours: overexposing yourself to the news on radio or TV or indulging in something that makes you laugh and lifts your spirits.

Some more ideas for having a good laugh:

- Play with your pet
- Watch funny films and comedy shows
- Be silly
- Tell or listen to good stories
- Get in touch with your inner child and play
- Video-record yourself dancing with your friends
- Attend a laughter workshop
- Make plenty of time for social, fun activities such as bowling or karaoke
- Simply think back on things that made you laugh out loud in the past

Smile Often—Be Radiant the Spiritual Way!

The chances you will attract nice people and opportunities into your life by always looking grumpy are pretty slim. Smiling often is not only important for your happiness and self-confidence; it does wonders for your health too! You don't have to fake it, nor do you need to show all your teeth, just gently smile as you go about your business. Alone or surrounded by many, smiling will make you shine. It will instantly change your mood and people will notice it.

The best makeup is a smile.

If you don't like looking shy or tired, try smiling more often. It will immediately change the way you look. Your aura will change too, and that's something else people will feel. Smiling gives you a certain feeling of control. When I am sad, I can deal with the situation better and more quickly if I smile. It allows me to take a step back and look at my circumstances from a lighter perspective. It gives me strength and clarity.

By smiling, I take charge of myself. I show the Universe that I am strong enough to deal with it and that I appreciate the learning experience. A very poignant example of this was my grandad's funeral. He was such an important person in my life, and I loved him very much. During the funeral, I had a choice: joining the sadness or not. I ***decided*** not to. Not there. Instead, I put a gentle smile on my face. I thought of all the great things about him and that he was now free from pain. I smiled thinking back on the memories we shared and how much time we used to spend together, and I was grateful. That day smiling really helped me to deal with my feelings and everything that was going on around me. By smiling more you help to light up your life and the lives of those around you.

Be More Playful

Your soul wants you to have fun! So go on and enjoy your life to the max! Grab any opportunity that will bring you more joy and happiness. All too often, we have to be so serious, responsible, perfect and impeccable. How about giving ourselves a break!

Be more playful, creative, wild, young and silly. Have you become too serious or even too spiritual to be playful? Please know that you can still be playful and have a great time while being responsible as well.

Tip: Watch children play!

We can learn so much from watching children play. They are free; their minds have not been influenced by the norms and rules of society in the way ours have. Notice their creativity, spontaneity, the drama, the passion, the imagination, the forgiveness, the sharing. Their imagination knows no limits. They are not concerned about money or comfort issues. Children dream out loud and speak their truth. Do you allow your inner child to play? Is there time for fun and creativity in your life?

Question to ask yourself: Do I allow myself to play and dream enough?

You can discover more about a person in an hour of play than in a year of conversation.

Plato

Avoid Goals That Put You Under Pressure

Goals can be very effective when you want to achieve certain things. They give you a clear concept of what you wish to obtain and help us to better manage our time, and give us the motivation we need.

Goal setting is particularly big in the field of coaching. Life and other coaches assist their clients in goal setting and then create action plans to achieve those goals. Personally (and I am a coach!) I believe that setting goals should come with a word of caution. If we set goals for ourselves that put too much pressure on us, what's the fun in even trying to achieve them? You may get to the finish, but if it leaves you feeling drained and exhausted, why bother? Make sure that your goals are inspiring and achievable.

We've all heard the story of the bride who spends more than a year preparing for her big day, only to fall ill during her honeymoon caused by the body de-stressing after what has been a very intense time.

When do teachers fall ill? That's right, during the holidays!

When do businessmen have a heart attack? On board an aircraft!

You see, the human body is only able to cope with a certain amount of stress. It "forces" you to slow down once in a while so that it can restore its energy levels.

When I decided to write this, my first book, I was very excited, but also a little anxious at the same time. I knew it would be a smart move to have it published sooner rather than later so that I could offer it to people during my lectures and seminars. My own mentors said what the book should look like, how many pages, what the topics should be, and so on. Soon the whole adventure became so daunting that I was honesty ready to dismiss the idea altogether. But then I thought, "Hang on a minute! Here's my chance to practice what I preach!" I knew I had to make the "goal" more inspiring for myself first. And that's when I came up with the vision I needed to keep myself focused during the many hours of writing: I pictured people ***enjoying*** reading my book and ***learning*** from it. Now that's a goal that motivated me! I could ask for nothing more than people enjoying my work and using the ideas to create a better life for themselves.

Are you expecting too much from yourself? Are your goals too stressful? Are you too attached to a certain result? If so, you may wish to review your goals. Make sure they are fun, inspirational, and above all, achievable for you. Different people have different skills, means and capacities. Yes, it is good to aim high in life, but make sure you ***enjoy the process***. Save some energy to reap the rewards of your efforts!

Now is a good time to be your own life coach!

Questions to ask yourself:

- What brings me joy?
- What is missing in my life?
- What needs to happen in order to get it?
- Realistically, what would be a great first step to get this?
- How can I add value to my life?
- How can I add value to other people's lives?

Always See the Beauty of the Moment

The past is gone.
The future is not yet here.
All there really is, is the now.

So much valuable time and energy are wasted on dwelling on the past or thinking about the future. I hear people say, "My life was better when...", "When I had..., I was happy", "If only I had..., then my life would be good" or "One day I will...." But "one day" may never come, so why waste all your time on something that may never happen?

The now, however, is all we can be certain about. Now is when we can take action. If you are not happy with your current situation, ask yourself, "What is one thing I could do now to change things?" and "How can I experience more joy in this very moment?"

Every single second of your life is important in its own right. Sure, some moments will be far more spectacular than others, but every moment in your life is a new opportunity to be inspired and to create and to take action. Making the shift from worrying about your past and future to focusing on the present moment can cause a dramatic improvement in your enjoyment of life, which we are all entitled to.

It was with high expectations that I embarked on my trip to the lost city of the Incas, Machu Picchu, in Peru. I had decided to make my thirtieth birthday one to remember forever, so I travelled alone to the other side of the planet to spend 11 days in this beautiful country. If you want to visit just one sacred place in your life, make sure to visit Machu Picchu; this site has been named one of the New Seven Wonders of the World, and I promise it will take your breath away. Being the "spiritual person" that I am, I had very high expectations in terms of receiving psychic guidance from the spirit world. Surely if I travelled all the way to this sacred place for a whole afternoon of meditation, Spirit would be kind enough to whisper in my ear and give me all sorts of visions for my future, right? That's what I thought at least. Guess what happened?

Nothing!

Yes, I will forever remember the view over Machu Picchu I had from where I was meditating (it's too beautiful to describe), but there were no voices of any kind talking to me whatsoever. I have to say that maybe I was a little bit disappointed...at first.

And then it hit me: In a moment of pure clarity, I had the realisation that everything that I will ever need in my life was already present in my life, at least to some extent. All that I really needed was to use the now to plant the seeds of my future. Suddenly, I understood that the now was a great time to explore options, possibilities, dreams and goals. That moment I was made aware that my life was perfect and that perfection can be found in the now, even when we so often think that our current situation is not good enough yet, and that true happiness is a thing of the past or future.

So, it turned out the Universe was with me after all on that day at Machu Picchu, and I felt that my connection with it was stronger than ever. I was gently but surely made aware that we needn't journey to the other side of the Earth to "escape" and to find the answers to our most pressing questions. What it all comes down to is to slow down once in a while. Indeed, sometimes we need to slow down in order to speed up.

Do you find yourself thinking about your past or future too often? Would it be helpful to you if you felt more present in the "now"?

Meditation is an invaluable practice when you quickly want to calm your mind, and it doesn't have to take long. Allow yourself one or two minutes to meditate and you'll reap immense rewards.

Here's a meditation technique my clients find very helpful:

- Find a space where you can be alone for two minutes. (If you're at work, go and sit in your car or the bathroom; you can even hide in a meeting room and shut the blinds. Be creative.)
- Then close your eyes. (Did you know that when you close your eyes, even for a little while, your brain wants to go into "sleeping mode"? No wonder it's so relaxing.)
- Take three deep breaths, inhaling for seven seconds and exhaling for eleven seconds. Imagine your lungs being filled with clear, cleansing air. Visualise exhaling all negative thoughts. See them dissolve into the Universe.
- Imagine a line coming down from the top of your head, down your body and eventually reaching your feet. You may see it swaying, much like your busy mind. Now as you calm your mind further, imagine the line slowly but surely coming to a standstill. When it has stopped moving completely, enjoy this tranquil moment.
- Thank yourself and the Universe for a lovely meditation.
- Some clients prefer to visualise a feather slowly drifting down over the duration of a couple of minutes until it lands between their feet. As always, be creative. You could imagine holding a baby until it falls asleep, or feel a butterfly landing and then resting on the top of your head. The aim is to quickly shift your focus from feeling overwhelmed and stressed to feeling grounded again in the present moment, for the now is really all there is.

Please don't be concerned that focusing on the present moment will hinder you from achieving long-term goals. In fact, it is quite the opposite. When our happiness only depends on succeeding in our goals, too much stress is caused. Therefore, I recommend you focus on the now and enjoy the process of working toward your dreams. Let your inner light guide you during this time of powerful creation. Consciously live every moment, every step of the way, be fully present, and before you know it, you will have arrived at your long-term goals, much quicker and with much more joy than you had expected.

Even giants take baby steps.

Make Sure There's a Balance in Giving & Receiving

You give so much, you share so much,
often from the heart, sometimes for gain.
But for a loving person like you, it's all the same.

But remember, it is good to know
that allowing yourself to receive
will truly make you grow.

This poem literally poured out of my hands as soon I wrote the tile for this topic. That's what happens when you connect to your inner light; you open the floodgates to a wealth of information, beauty, creativity and inspiration. When you are in that place of truth, you are very "accessible" for guidance from the Universe, and often it will infuse you with wisdom and fresh ideas; you'll receive the motivation and insight that's right for you at that moment in time.

Are you someone who "gives" all the time? Do you always say "yes" to anything people ask you to do? Are you always making sure that things go well for others? Do you spend hours counselling a friend on the phone when in fact you are tired and would rather be doing other things?

It's normal for spiritually-oriented people to be "givers" and therefore it's important for them to find a ***balance*** in giving and receiving. Yes, the Universe likes us to treat each other well, but please understand that allowing yourself to receive is an essential step towards personal and spiritual growth. You are, in fact, disrespectful to your soul if you always deny it to receive.

Are you always ready to pay the bill at the restaurant before someone else has had the chance to get their wallet out? If so, you may need to ask yourself, "Why do I always do this?" Is it because you like the attention? Do you think people will like you more if you pay for them every time? Two things are going on here: First of all, you will never receive if you don't let others give to you, and secondly, you are stopping your friends' own growth by denying them the opportunity to give anything back.

We all want other people to treat us well, but when this happens, we often run away as if our life depended on it. Why is it so difficult to let people treat us well? We say, "Oh no, I am fine, thanks" rather than ***accepting*** something we are being given. We seem to cope better, however, when there's some kind of exchange involved, which is, obviously, money most of the time. We book ourselves in for a massage because we can pay for it, which seems to make it easier. But when someone brings us flowers to thank us for something we've done, we say, "Oh, you shouldn't have" or "That's nice, but it's too much! I can't accept that" or anything along those lines. Yet when we accept a gift from someone, we give that person the opportunity to open up and experience the joy of giving.

My clients feel so much lighter once they finally learn to let go of this "giving-all-the-time" habit. This shift happens when you learn how to receive without feeling guilty.

So, the next time someone offers you a free meal or a drink, or they give you a huge compliment, say, "Thank you very much!" and then wholeheartedly accept that gift.

Use Positive Feedback to do More of What You do Well

A great way to discover your path in life is to listen carefully for feedback people give you. I am not talking about the kind of feedback you get at the office but real-life feedback, such as the comments and suggestions people around you give to you. This feedback comes from the heart and can inspire and encourage you to take action.

Pay special attention to "throw-away" comments from your friends. "You have always been good at helping people" and "You ought to look into developing your painting talents more" are examples of quick, but significant, suggestions that can be extremely valuable.

When people give you these kinds of caring comments, it means you did something that connected you to your inner light. That is why you did it so well and it was noticed.

Do you get positive feedback from your friends? If yes, do you shy away and say, "Oh, thanks, but you know...." or do you use it as a compass to help you do more things in life that you are naturally good at?

A couple of years ago, I was approached by the director of a major spiritual centre in London to host a seminar. When I emailed him a draft proposal of content for the seminar, he replied to me saying, "I love the way you write. You write like you speak. Could you send me some articles on spirituality, and we will publish them in our monthly newsletter?"

Until that moment, it was never my intention to become a writer. I had written some articles for my website, but never thought of becoming a "published" author. But his feedback made me realise that I was doing something right and I began to explore this "hidden talent".

I was really pleased that I did take his suggestion on board and soon discovered the immense joy—and potential to spread my wings further—of writing from the heart.

Forgive Yourself

One of the biggest obstacles that keeps us from moving forward and living a happy life is guilt. Learning to let go of guilt is one of the things I enjoy helping my clients with the most. Guilt stunts your growth; it makes you feel awful, disempowered and weak.

If you are one of those people who often feel guilty, here's a tip I want to share with you and I know it will help you: Only feel guilty when you did something with deliberate intent to hurt someone.

All other outcomes that make you feel guilty and are not done with your intention to hurt or offend someone, ***let them go.*** Whenever the guilt gremlin appears and nags at your conscience, simply ask yourself, "Was it my intention to hurt this person?" or "Was it my intention to cause damage?" If the answer is an honest "no" then respect yourself enough to let go of guilt. It's a feeling you are better off without.

If you did do something that was not quite right, you can still deal with it in order to become happy and lighter again. Take responsibility for your actions, and apologise to the person you've hurt, if necessary. The more authentic you become and the more you respect yourself, the easier it is to let go of guilt.

Have you taken something that wasn't yours? Have you done something that wasn't nice? Have you said something to upset someone? Take a deep breath and relax. Make a conscious decision to make things right. Think how much better you'll feel when you can let go of the guilt.

What a relief it will be! Stop beating yourself up for what happened in the past. Deal with your guilt demon, and walk towards a future of relief and piece of mind. You can do it!

It is NEVER 'too late' to make things 'right'.
It can't be. Both 'time' and 'right' are illusions.
You have complete freedom.
Take responsibility and step into your power.

So, if you want to 'undo' the past, create your future by focusing on what you can do well. Now.

Create a Sacred Space in Your Home, Just for You

Okay, you can relax. I am not talking here about turning your house into a Zen temple. But if you would like to create that special ambiance and have some well-deserved you time, it would be useful to have a space in your house where you can go to meditate and relax. Just imagine that sacred spot where you can truly be yourself and develop your spiritual side.

It's easy to turn any ordinary room into your own special place: a few candles, your favourite incense, some gentle music in the background, a picture you love, and any other items that are special to you.

You can set up the room in a short time and then do a meditation or simply sit quietly and enjoy the time out for yourself. Switch off your phone and make sure you will not be disturbed. It's in these moments of peace and quiet that you have a perfect opportunity to connect to your inner light and reflect on your current situation. As you centre yourself, you will become more relaxed and inspired. Listen carefully to the guidance you may receive from your subconscious mind as well.

I recommend that you do these short meditations often. Before you know it, you won't want to miss them for anything, and you'll automatically slot your meditation time into your busy agenda.

You may choose to put your relaxation items away when you have finished or leave them permanently so that the room is always ready for you to retreat to.

When you connect to your inner light; you open the floodgates to a wealth of information, beauty, creativity and inspiration.

Create Your Treasure Chest

I often ask clients, "How would you feel if you had something you could turn to for instant peace of mind when you are feeling stressed or upset?"

I call this creating your treasure chest. Find yourself a nice box (or a simple shoe box will do; you can always decorate it) in which you can keep all sort of things that are precious to you: a favourite holiday picture, a souvenir, a letter from a loved one, a brochure from your favourite concert, a drawing from your godchild, a gemstone, an entrance ticket to a museum, a ticket to your first West End show, an airline boarding pass from a special holiday, and so forth. Make sure to put in any messages you have received with positive feedback or praise for you such as cards and letters. Make this box your "treasure chest", your special place in your own house where you can go to at any time for a quick boost of reassurance, calmness and feel-good therapy. I can't remember exactly how many "thank-you" emails I have received from clients after I told them this simple but wonderful tip.

Another suggestion is to create a folder in your email inbox on your work computer and give it a special name, such as "Success", "Good", "Love" or "Smile" (any positive label). In this inbox folder keep all the emails that made you feel good in the past. They can be positive feedback from your supervisor, a lovely note from a colleague, a "thank-you" message from a satisfied customer, and, of course, any good joke emails that are worth keeping. My email folder at work used to be called "Success!" and I absolutely loved adding new emails to it!

Having your special email folder or box is a great way of giving yourself a quick boost. When you are having a not-so-nice day, all you need to do is quickly browse through all those positive and funny emails to shift your emotion from bad to good.

Like I have said so many times before, growing spiritually is not just about striving for enlightenment. It's also about making small, but significant, changes in your everyday lifestyle to make you feel better and lighten your burden.

Praise Yourself

I want you to take a moment now and do this short exercise: Make a list of at least five things that you've done particularly well during the past three days in your journal or below. Think carefully about what you have really excelled at lately and what made you feel proud of yourself.

Examples:

- ***"I praise myself for spending extra time being there for my friend."***
- ***"I praise myself for doing a really good workout at the gym yesterday."***
- ***"I praise myself for helping my friend move house."***
- ***"I praise myself for doing the grocery shopping for my grandad."***

Exercise: I praise myself for:

1. ______________________________
2. ______________________________
3. ______________________________
4. ______________________________
5. ______________________________

If you struggle to write down even a few things you can praise yourself for, it's a sign you're not ***valuing*** yourself enough. You may think you're not good enough yet to deserve praise, but if not now, when? If you can't say something good about yourself, why would others do it? First and foremost, you must recognise all the good that ***you*** do and praise yourself for it, before expecting others to praise you.

It's okay and important to say something good about yourself; by doing so, you honour your inner light that shines so brightly in you, wanting to be recognised. Pat yourself on the back; you deserve it!

Spiritualty for Rat Racers

Is it possible to combine spirituality with everyday life? Of course! And the great thing is that it won't cost you any of your precious time. Welcoming spirituality into your life does not require that you spend all of your free time on soul searching and reading about spiritual matters or self-help books. Nor does it require hours of meditation or attending gatherings with like-minded people. Becoming more spiritually aware is a wonderful pathway that's open for you to explore, in your own time, without any pressure. You decide how far you wish to journey, and remember, you don't have to be religious to be spiritual!

So here we are, waking up at six in the morning and then rushing around all day. Many of us don't get home until 12 hours later. It's madness! With a thousand and one things to do and with ever-increasing expectations from society, for many people life is simply becoming too stressful and overwhelming. Some of us may feel trapped in the rat race and are looking for a way out, or at least a way to slow down. Many of the options available however, such as drugs, food abuse and retail therapy, are far from beneficial and can lead to even more stress and unhappiness.

This is where spirituality comes in. It has all the potential to alleviate much of this daily stress and to help you calm down on many levels. It can help you see the wood for the trees and recharge your batteries. This new supply of energy will help you soar higher than ever before, with a new sense of clarity and purpose that you had only imagined possible. It will bring new situations, opportunities and people your way as if by magic, so why not welcome spirituality into your life? Let it take you on a wonderful journey of self-discovery, healing and growth. It really is possible, and here are just a few tips:

- Raise your level of awareness. Ask yourself these questions: "How ready am I to bring about changes in my life?", "How will spirituality assist me on my path?" and "What is my path?" Do you know of friends who are already into alternative therapies and meditation, or who enjoy movies and literature with a deeper meaning? As you raise your level of awareness, you will start to notice that spirituality is not some far-away concept, but is all around you and much more available and accessible to you than you might realise.
- Express your gratitude. As often as possible, say silently or out loud: "I am so grateful for this experience", "This makes me feel so good inside", "That meeting gave me an opportunity to shine", "This traffic jam gives me time to enjoy my favourite music", "I am happy that I was able to help that person" or "I am so grateful to have a job". Spirituality has got nothing to do with religion, so rather than thanking a higher being you can express your gratitude to yourself. If you do this often enough, you will create an overall feeling of self-empowerment and contentment.
- Value yourself and be gentle on yourself. As I mentioned earlier using positive affirmations to feel better about yourself is very worthwhile. It is so easy to do and requires very little practice. Affirmations are powerful statements that you can use to boost the way you feel about yourself. Used regularly, they will help you to change limiting thoughts and beliefs. Unfortunately, most people use negative affirmations such as "I am too fat", "I'm not good enough", "I don't deserve this" or "I am so stupid". Because of this, they undermine their self-esteem and self-worth. Positive affirmations, on the other hand, carry a positive message that empower you and quite simply make you feel better. Here are some examples

that you can start using straight away: "I look forward to inspiring people today", "I am safe", "I trust my inner guidance", "I allow miracles to come to me", "I attract abundance", "I have so much to offer to the world" and "I am becoming more of who I want to be every day". When it comes to "having" and "needing" in life, be gentler on yourself. Instead of saying, "I have to go to the gym" and "I need to change my diet" replace them with "I choose to go the gym" and "I decide to change my diet". You are always in the driver's seat and you have more control of your life than you think. And if it doesn't always feel that way, then use positive affirmations to instantly remind you of that.

No matter how busy your life is, there might be more room available to open yourself up to spirituality than you are aware of. Be gentle with yourself, and start with small but significant steps towards exploring the information that awaits you. It may reach you in different ways and formats. You can use the techniques mentioned above or simply acknowledge and then express your desire to attract more spirituality into your life, and it ***will*** come your way. Allow it all in and don't resist the flow of information. Remember, being truly spiritual means valuing yourself and following your own inner guidance. From all the information on spirituality that comes your way, ***take what resonates and leave the rest.***

Have fun with it. Discover how easy it is to combine a busy lifestyle with personal and spiritual growth. You will soon discover how much easier your life becomes because of this growth.

Be in a Job That Helps You Grow as a Person

Few things upset me more than the way most people feel about their job. I once used to know someone who was only in his twenties but was already dreaming about his retirement; I think I never quite got over that. I will never understand why people count down to the weekend, either. If you only live for the weekend, that means you are basically "dying" for five days, no? Judging from the look on some people's faces and their posture that might just be the case! I am not trying to be smart here, and I know we all have bills to pay, but I do find it strange how so many people simply "accept" any job in order to make a living. "But I like the people" or "It pays well" or "One day I will find myself a job I really like" is what people say to convince themselves. But your colleagues may leave and "one day" may never come, so if you are going to spend eight hours of your day doing a job, don't you think it would be good to find one that's actually fulfilling—a job that makes you happy and brings you real satisfaction, rather than just a paycheck?

There's an important spiritual teaching that says, "Work and pray". The first time I read this, years ago, I was a little disappointed and I remember thinking to myself: "Gosh, that's a bit strict." But as I developed my spiritual side, I came to understand what it really means. In "Work and pray" "Work" refers to doing something that brings you ***joy*** and is constructive at the same time. "Another day, another dollar" is a saying you won't hear from someone who's in a job that's genuinely exciting. People who are really passionate about their position don't see their job as "work" but as a great opportunity to use their skills and talents.

I remember when I was still in high school I promised myself that I would never be in a job I wouldn't absolutely love. And I haven't. The jobs I've been in have taken me around the globe more than five times over, to every continent, and have allowed me to interact with the most interesting people from different cultures and backgrounds. You see, that's what I mean, find yourself a job you love! I left university because I knew it wasn't for me. I had a passion for the airline industry, and I thought it would be great to be a part of it. Next thing I knew, I was seeing the world, earning a very good salary, and really enjoying myself. When the accumulation of jet lag finally got the better of me, I decided it was time to pursue another dream of mine: to become a teacher. And, again staying true to my dream as a teenager of never being in a dead-end job, I did. It was the teaching job that really opened up many new and exciting possibilities for me. I began putting my own teaching materials together and designed various courses.

Not only did this lead to a wonderful promotion at work, but more importantly, it allowed me to develop my public speaking and presentation skills, which I now use on a daily basis, doing coaching sessions and international workshops and seminars. Again, your job is what you make of it, literally.

If you sit around, drumming your fingers, you'll be waiting forever for that promotion or bonus. But if you decide today to become proactive, connect to your inner light, and start using your innate talents, you'll soon be enjoying a new job and the respect from your managers and colleagues, and more importantly, yourself.

Take a New Look at Money Issues

You are more than your mind and your body. You are, in essence, a soul. Millions upon millions of years ago, we were born from the Source (***All That Is, God,*** etc) in order for us to gain experience through our soul's journey. This journey transpires over millions of years and many lifetimes, taking on many different life forms, from primitive to very advanced. As a human being on planet Earth, a soul can really accelerate its growth. That is why most, but not all, souls decide to incarnate on our planet. Our world provides many wonderful opportunities for our soul to blossom. Many "good" and "bad" things happen to us, and we are constantly challenged by life. By living consciously we can move out of playing the victim role.

Spirituality can be very useful in times like these, when money is tight. The media are always feeding us bad news, and the pressure to stay in control and look fabulous is stronger than ever. We can start to wonder what life is all about and why we should give so much when we get so little back. Realising that you are more than what you see in the mirror is the key to dealing with life's challenges. Remember, you are a soul and not just a name in a passport. You chose to be here in order to experience as much as possible to nurture your very essence. Now that you know that, take a look at your life now.

See how the things that "happen" to you are more than just nasty situations. They are vital learning opportunities. Embrace them. Each lifetime you have is a new opportunity, not a duty, to get it right.

If you sit still and are scared to make "mistakes" you slow down your soul's growth. If you put too much pressure on yourself and beat yourself up, there's a good chance you will need longer to "graduate" from the university that is life.

Many of my coaching clients come to me to talk about money related stress issues. As a spiritual coach, I often share with them my view on what we really are and why we are here. When my clients "get" this and realise that they own a beautiful soul, they begin to feel a wonderful sense of responsibility for looking after this soul, which is, after all, the core of their "beingness".

They start to feel a lot lighter and in charge of their life. Their perspectives on their circumstances begin to change, and their heart is filled with joy. This joy comes from understanding that they can fulfil the very reason for being here on this planet. For when they embrace the challenges in their life, rather than reject them, they will contribute to their souls' mission.

So remember that you are, in each lifetime, an expression of your soul. And your soul keeps coming back to perfect itself. It is a very conscious choice. Remember, you are a part of God, for you were born from the Source, but it was ***you*** who decided to ***experience*** life. It was not something you had to do. No one made you take on this lifetime, and no one, except you (in your very role as God), will decide how fruitful the journey has been, and move on from there.

So do live your life to the full. You have every right to do so. There is no point in exhausting yourself copying others who seemingly have more than you do. They don't. It is their soul that chooses to experience wealth. It can be more taxing than you think.

Now, if you understand what I've been saying and you appreciate how the current economic climate provides us with learning opportunities, you may wish to try the following: Speak to your soul when you have a moment of peace and quiet. Consult with your true essence and tell it you feel ready to progress in life. Express your desire to embrace more wealth and happiness. Maybe your soul is now ready to do just that. But it will need your permission. You are always in control.

Have fun with this.... You can begin right now by asking yourself: "How will my soul be affected if I stay stuck in my current circumstances?" and "What can I do today to make my soul smile?"

Thinking abundantly and giving thanks for all the wonderful things in your life can help you to attract more abundance into your life, whether it's financial abundance or an abundance of love and happiness. What we focus on we attract more of, so believing you are wealthy can help to create more wealth into your life. Why not try it now and enjoy the process?

Be Less Defensive

Don't you get tired of people who immediately fire any random remark back at you after you've tried to ask them a polite question that may show that you have a different view from theirs? I do. It's simply annoying when people are defensive. They think they are smart, but in fact by acting in this manner, they display their weakness and inability to communicate properly. Being defensive is one way of being a mirror reflecting back to ourselves our fear of perhaps not being good enough, so we always have to prove that we are right. It is important to think before we speak; we are not always right, and sometimes we make mistakes, and it is through them that we have the opportunity to learn. Here's a little secret that will help you achieve just that: ***Learn to listen first***. Even if you are not too keen on the topic of discussion, rather than being defensive and saying any old thing, just for the sake of being heard and proving you are right, be patient and be a good listener first.

Respect Others and Appreciate That They Are Entitled to Their Own Beliefs

During my coaching sessions, many clients admit they want to change their spouse, friends, parents, managers and so on. They believe that many of their issues will be solved if only the other person would change. By assuming their issues are caused by "other people" they spend much time and energy trying to change them, usually to no avail.

Do you like it when people try to change your beliefs? No? Then why try changing theirs? The only one you need to focus on is you. Each soul is unique and is entitled to his or her own values and beliefs. Please know that respecting people and their opinions does not mean you have to agree with them, it is simply a case of accepting them as they are.

Are you ready to invite wonderful personal and professional relationships into your life without having to agree on everything? It's easier than you think. You don't have to change who you are, and you don't have to become a pushover either. When you explain, rather than instruct, what you believe in, people will begin to listen to you and appreciate you.

Question to ask yourself: Why do I feel the need to force my beliefs onto someone?

Use Your Power Wisely

Are you a strong person? Of course, by that, I mean ***energetically*** strong, not physically. Have you got a powerful aura? Are you one of those people who command respect and make others fall silent as soon as you enter the room? Do people follow you blindly and look up to you? It's okay to be a leader and be powerful. If it's the way you are and the way people react to you, accept it. Striving for the highest good for yourself and other people is beneficial to all.

Please keep in mind that it's smart to use your power wisely. Use the power given to you by the Universe to inspire other people, to coach them, support them, and to create opportunities for them. Involve other people in your life and work. When they may be finding life a challenge, share with them how it is that you can be so "powerful". Being lovingly powerful is a characteristic of great leaders who have inspired many souls. You too can do this, especially those of you who are in supervisory roles at work or in organisations where there is the opportunity to help other people develop, rather than create a gap between you and your subordinates. Courses on leadership and communication skills are an incredibly valuable investment, and you may want to check whether any are being conducted near you.

Use your Universe-given power wisely—it will get you very far, indeed.

Questions to ask yourself: How does my energy affect other people? Do people feel better or worse after talking to me?

Give a Compliment to at Least One Person Every Day

Make giving a compliment to at least one person every day a habit. It's such a great way to make others feel fantastic, and because giving compliments feels good, it'll help you along as well. Moreover, if the compliment is genuine, you will be valued and appreciated more. It's a win-win situation!

Again, make sure your compliments are valid. No one benefits from hearing you say, "I love your shoes" when all you want to do is throw them out of the window. Or "You are a brilliant singer" when, in fact, your eardrums are bleeding! They key is to be authentic.

You may want to give compliments like these:

- ***"You know, I have always valued .... in you."***
- ***"Doing .... is one of the things that makes you really special."***
- ***"If it wasn't for your ..., we wouldn't be this successful."***
- ***"I trust you so much, because you... "***
- ***"I wanted to say how much I appreciate it when you...; it makes me feel..."***

When you give a compliment in this way, it will come across as sincere and respectful. And it sounds so much better than the usual, "Oh, I like your..." Also, learn to give ***yourself*** a compliment. If you think that's a little weird, begin with congratulating yourself, even for the smallest things you do. Whenever you've done something particularly well, tell yourself, "Well done, you!"

Whether you let someone go ahead of you at checkout, send someone a card to tell them how much you value their friendship, or help a young mother carry her shopping bags, say to yourself, "Well done, you" or "That was nice of you to do". You're not going crazy by talking to yourself, by the way. We all do it! The problem is that we talk ourselves down too often. So the next time you do something really well, give yourself a compliment, because you deserve it. Believe me, it's a very healthy and powerful way to boost your self-esteem.

***You are beautiful. You are me.
I am beautiful. I am you.
We are beautiful. We are the Universe. The Universe is beautiful. It is us. The power of connection is as weak as the strength of individuality. My heart is my power. You are in it. Your power is in the heart.***

Follow Your Dreams, or They Will Follow You

One of my all-time favourite artists, the wonderful and highly talented singer Sarah Brightman, once said in an interview: "It is my experience that, when you ignore an instinct, you will reach a moment where you will go back to it anyway." I have always believed in this truth. Your dreams are often the creative extension of your instincts. They are like the G.P.S. in your car; if you are heading in the wrong direction, sooner or later you will be prompted to turn around and follow a different route.

Even though I know we experience life on Earth for the evolution of our soul, and therefore we are faced with certain challenges, it would be crazy to think that there's only one way to reach our dreams. Is your car satellite navigation system always showing you the one way to your destination? Of course not. We can choose to ignore it and try to find our own route, but it may take us longer and we might become frustrated. However, we always have choice. We have the choice to embrace the challenges in life or to ignore them. Either way is up to us.

When we "graduate" from this lifetime, we'll have the chance to review how well we have dealt with those challenges. There will be no judgment from anyone. But, of course, we will want to enjoy looking back on our life, and that means seeing how well we handled it all, "good" and "bad" alike. So now that you know this, would you not want to consider getting it right this time around? You have created this lifetime for yourself, so why not acknowledge the decision of your soul to birth here and embrace life, with all its extremes.

Of course, this includes your dreams. For many people daring to trust their dreams and then following them is the greatest challenge they will ever face, for dreams are not always easy to bring to life. Understanding, accepting, constructing, following, and then later manifesting our dreams, often demands a lot of courage and dedication.

The creative process can be a very lonely path as well. Before I started working with my first coaching clients, and long before the first groups of guests came to my seminars, I spent an awful lot of time on my own, working day and night on all my different projects. I didn't mind though because I knew it would get me to where I wanted to be. Yes, you may have to miss out on the parties, the barbeques, the nights out and so on, but if you know deep inside that you need the time to manifest your projects, then go for it. There's an added benefit to all this too: You learn to appreciate your own company!

Follow your dreams. Take a risk and live the life you have always wanted.

PART 2:
Top 10 Questions My Clients Ask Me

When you arrive at the crossroads of life,
your life coach is there to help you choose the right exit,
and follow the road ahead.

My coaching clients come to me with a variety of issues, goals and challenges. However, there are certain questions that always seem to come back, and I want to take this opportunity to share them with you here. Not only because the information will be helpful to you, but you'll also see that you are not the only one who has these issues on their mind.

So many people out there are looking for answers to their questions, but only strong people like you, who are ***ready*** to enhance the quality of their life and empower themselves, actively seek guidance to learn how they can connect to their inner light.

Here are my answers to the "Top 10" frequently asked questions by the people I work with, be it during one-to-one sessions or coaching seminars and lectures. You will find that I've touched upon many of the answers already in this book. This is because the more you read or hear something, the easier it will stick in your mind.

1. "How can I feel lighter?"

The Number One Question is, in fact, a non-spoken question. Very often, people who come to me may not precisely know what they want to talk about, or what they wish to work on, but they do know one thing: they wish to feel lighter. I really pride myself on offering something that's vastly different from other life coaches: I don't work with a specific coaching target market, I work with people from all walks of life. Practical spirituality underpins what I do, but the coaching agenda can be about anything my clients wish to discuss. This allows for a much more holistic approach. After all, many topics are important to people in life, so why not use the coaching session as your opportunity to discuss them? My work is not just for 'women over 40 wishing to build better relationships with attractive young men' or for 'new single dads looking to become excellent golf players'. I can see how having a set coaching target market might work for other coaches in terms of streamlining their business resources, but thankfully, that's not how it works for me. That would be like saying to the Universe: "I only feel like enjoying my life on Wednesdays, all other days mean nothing to me."

I have the privilege of working with people from different backgrounds and cultures. It fills my heart with joy to see that they feel intrigued by the spiritual undertone in my work, yet at the same time there is no coaching "threshold" that might scare them from approaching someone in the first place. Strong construction workers, sensitive housewives, flamboyant hairdressers, successful business men, managers, team leaders or even other spiritual workers – often come to a coaching session with me and when they sit down and I ask: "How are you? What would you like to talk about today", or "How can I be there for you?" This is usually followed, not by a straightforward answer, but by a moment of quiet reflection and often even an emotional release. You see, people can't always put their finger on the "one issue" that causes an imbalance in their life. Often there are many aspects that are playing a role, and people simply want to be heard sometimes. They wish to feel lighter first, and have some breathing space to gain clarity, and then work on other issues later on, feeling inspired and energised.

Here are three suggestions to help you start feeling lighter in the shortest possible time:

1. Create time for what you really like. I am sure that a lot of the stress you may have in your life comes from simply not being able to do that what you enjoy doing most. If you are completely inundated with work or when your family depends on you 24/7, there's usually not much time left over for hobbies, exercise or your social life. Feeling lighter and happier comes when we have enough time for ourselves to do the things that nourish our soul. So, take away the opportunities to do those things that make you happy, and it's no surprise you'll feel something is missing in your life. Do whatever it takes to create more time for you. Indulge in your hobbies and the things that bring you joy; it's so important and you are certainly entitled to it! If you keep telling yourself "One day it will be better" and "One day I'll have more time", let me tell you that after "one day" there will be another day that will also keep you busy and distracted from what you would rather be

doing. I would like to ask you this question: "What can you do today to create more time for yourself in life?" If you struggle to answer this question, take a moment now to connect to your inner light. When you listen carefully, the answer will soon reveal itself.

2. Be more authentic. Use the tips you've learned in this book to help you become more you. By authentic, I mean start living in alignment with your own values and beliefs, not those from society. It's good to be different. Follow your own dreams and goals and speak your truth; it's easier than you think, and will give you the power and motivation to create a lighter life. If you are "sick" of always pretending to be someone you're not, then being more of who you really are will "heal" you and allow you to feel whole.

The truth is sometimes uncomfortable, but always helpful.

3. Face your challenges. Recognise what causes you stress, and then decide to face those issues once and for all. Make a conscious decision to allow yourself to live a lighter life and approach someone, like a coach or mentor, who can help you achieve this. I strongly believe that facing your challenges and accepting them for what they are—challenges—will bring about the quickest progress. Any cursing, negative thinking or procrastinating will only lead to having those challenges in your life for longer than you want. Remember how we talked about going from victim to winner in your life? Take responsibility for anything that worries you. You may not have consciously chosen to have it on your plate, but you can certainly choose to face it, right here and right now. Make an inspired decision now to deal proactively with your challenges, and then commit to that decision. I always tell clients to keep a clear vision of how good they will feel once their issues have disappeared as a result of dealing with them head-on. Think of how great you'll feel when the problems are behind you.

2. *"How can I find my life purpose?"*

My biggest advice is to stop "looking". You won't find it anywhere out there, but ***within*** you. It makes me sad to see the pressure people put on themselves to find that "one-and-only" life purpose. The search for our life mission often causes us years of unnecessary worrying and disappointment. And what if you are good at many things? Have you considered that? You have to remember that your soul is here to experience life in order to grow. Simply being here on Earth and living your life the best you can is already ***good enough***, so you can let go of the pressure of finding your life purpose right here and right now. However, if you do feel that something is missing or that you want to spread your wings further, as always I strongly recommend that you connect to your inner light and pay close attention to your feelings. If there is something you are meant to be doing in your life, it will reveal itself to you sooner or later. This "Aha!" moment can come to you unexpectedly or can be the result of researching what you really like and feel inspired to do. What motivates you? Could you make a living out of it? Try out different things, and listen to what your inner guidance tells you. Let the light within you light your path to a fulfilling and meaningful life. Be gentle with yourself and ***enjoy*** the journey of self-discovery.

I remember Karen, a client from Belgium, who told me she'd given up on finding her life purpose. She said to me, "You know, it worries me that I can't seem to find the one thing I am supposed to do in my life, I seem to be good at many different things!"

"Then ***that's*** your purpose" I said.

"Really?" She asked, sounding excited but slightly puzzled.

"But it's not one specific thing!" She added.

"It's what makes you ***you***, and what makes you unique!" I reassured her.

"Embrace your many innate skills and talents. You would be surprised how many people wish they could multitask like you."

"I had never looked at it that way!" she told me, with a beaming smile on her face.

You see, that's the power of coaching: it helps you to look at things from a different angle, offering you a fresh perspective. It can be an incredibly moving experience, for it often lifts a huge weight off your shoulders.

There might be something you are good at, which may become your life purpose, rather than having a purpose you need to become good at.

3. "How can I learn to love myself more?"

Begin with learning to enjoy your own company. Do you find it hard to spend time on your own, even when you are busy? Not being able to spend time on our own often indicates not loving and appreciating ourselves enough. I recommend that the next time you are alone at home, keep the TV switched off and think about what you already like about yourself. What are you good at? Do you get praise from people for anything in particular? Take a look at those things, and love yourself for being great at them; don't just take this for granted. You have probably spent a lot of time honing your skills and talents, and it's natural and beneficial to enjoy the praise you get for this.

Example: I like to read thank-you letters I have received from clients, because they tell me I have done a good job. I know how much time and energy I have invested in setting up my coaching practice, and for that, I appreciate and love myself. This is healthy and nourishes the soul.

Respect yourself as you would do for the people you love. You buy them presents and give them compliments; you go out of your way for them and you forgive them if need be. Now start doing the same for yourself, and respect the beautiful soul that you truly are. Do you allow yourself nice things, or do you tell yourself that you are not good enough yet and don't deserve them? There's no need to spend a fortune on yourself, by the way. It's absolutely possible to respect yourself more by making small but important steps, such as taking some time out to go for a nice walk, or by allowing yourself to accept the help that people offer, rather than overloading yourself and getting exhausted.

We are all a part of the Universe. We are a body of energy and the Universe is energy, thus we are part of it. Now, if you replaced the word Universe with God, or a name that feels comfortable for you, you'll see that, in fact, you are a ***part*** of God. And would you say you respected the God Source? If so, have a guess what that means. If you love God and you are part of God, then you love yourself too. And you should! That inner light of yours is a spark of the God Source, and it is also your connection to it. It's a real shame that many people believe that God is "up there" and we are "only down here". The Universe is all around us and what the Universe, or God Source, really wants is for you to ***enjoy*** your life and ***love*** and ***respect*** yourself, not hide behind any silly misconceptions you may have about yourself. So the next time you are being disrespectful and unloving towards yourself, immediately banish those unconstructive feelings and remember that you are, indeed, God. Now that you know that, don't you agree the time is right to start loving yourself a lot more? I do!

"You are not your Thoughts", "You are not your Physical Body",

"You are not your Ego", … some teachers will say…

But I say you are ALL of that.

You ARE your Thoughts, you ARE your Body, and you ARE your Ego.

Who else do they belong to?

Yes, you are MORE than that, but in this human form

you are that what you chose to be.

Why do people fight with their Ego? Why do they hate their Minds?

Why do they dislike their Body, which they chose in the first place?

Why detach from elements that make you YOU?

They are an integral part of Who You Are.

Embrace them, don't curse them, for they are all part

of the Magnificent Energetic Being that you Are.

Embrace your Life. Embrace your Self.

Embrace the Extraordinary.

4. "How can I create wealth?"

Now that I have your attention…

Oh, the money issue! Is it any wonder that in today's world so many people approach a life coach to help them find ways to make extra cash or to deal with the stress caused by a lack of it? But creating wealth as a goal is too complex. It's very easy to see why many people get discouraged and give up.

First things first: I want you to define ***wealth.*** What does it actually mean to you? Just money… or is there more? Simply wanting "wealth" is just too vague to attract it into your life. And what are your beliefs about money? It's important that you check how you feel about money and if you believe you are worthy of receiving it, or else wealth may never come to you. I don't need you to believe in the law of attraction (a spiritual concept stating that like attracts like), but haven't you heard sayings such as "Money goes to money" and "The rich get richer and the poor get poorer"? There's a reason why people say these things. The Universe is always listening ***and*** obliging, so be careful with your beliefs about money and wealth.

Most of my clients come to me because they are seriously ready to create a happier and lighter life. And since the money and life purpose cards are so often on the proverbial coaching table, I always ask my clients if they have considered finding ways of turning their passion and dreams into a career. To my surprise, most hadn't or had quickly dismissed any wild dreams in that direction, fearing that they would never make a living from doing what they love. And so guess what happens? You're right: nothing. It's another clear example of how we sometimes block ourselves from becoming successful and living a fulfilling life. Let's face it: There's a perception that unless you're in a well-paid job, the chances of creating a financially wealthy life are slim. But maybe the thing that you dream of doing could be a well-paid job.

Keep in mind that if you want to start making money from your passion, it is absolutely essential that you believe it ***can*** be true for you. So if you are serious about this, you can always begin by taking baby steps first. You could look into going part-time at your current job and devote the rest of your time to making money, doing what makes your heart sing. If you are good at what you do, and you have the right beliefs to motivate and encourage you, the wealth you are looking for may well arrive soon. But if you don't try and you don't lock on to that inner light of yours, you'll never know.

Take a moment now to reflect on the following either below or in your journal:

Wealth to me means: ______________________

____

Now, what wealth *really* means to me is this:

____

____

____

These are my current beliefs about deserving wealth: ______________________

____

____

On a scale from 1 (low) to 10 (high), how much do I believe I can become wealthy: _____

Now ask yourself: What could I do ***today*** to increase that number if necessary? What am I good at? Could I use my innate skills and talents, which are part of my inner light, in a more lucrative way? Where could I find guidance to help me with this exciting goal?

A job gives you money,
but true wealth comes from following your dreams.

5. "How can I manage my stress?"

Stress is fantastic. That's providing you understand how to use stress as a compass rather than the negative energy that can make you sick or even kill you. Let me explain: By saying that stress is fantastic, I mean that it's a great tool (the compass) that will indicate whether you're on track or not. So rather than cursing the fact that you are stressed, and therefore causing yourself even more stress, take a moment now to appreciate how your stress is indeed the spiritual slap in your face that's needed to wake you up.

Investigate where your feelings of stress originate from. Can you tell me where exactly your stress comes from? What specifically causes you to feel drained and flat? In my experience of working with coaching clients, I have discovered that it's not their busy lifestyles that cause them stress; it's ***frustration.*** They are frustrated with themselves. People work so hard and seem to cope well with everything, but the one thing they can't cope with any longer is the fact that they are ignoring themselves. There simply is not enough time in their day or week to connect to their inner light. And when you don't follow the dreams of your soul, you become annoyed and frustrated, which leads to stress.

So when I'm asked what I suggest to manage stress, my answer is very simple: Respect yourself enough to draw a line under self-denial. Stop taking on more than you can handle, and look into ways of making time for yourself. Make a commitment to yourself that from now on you are going to allow yourself to live a lighter life. And that can only happen if you do more of what you want to do, say more of what you want to say, and be more of what you want to be. You will probably still be very busy, but you'll feel inspired and motivated, rather than stressed and drained.

Once you are serious about putting a halt to unhelpful stress, set up strong support systems to help you help yourself. This could include hiring a life coach, asking your friends to support you, becoming a member of a self-help group or organisation, and so forth. How many times have you told yourself that you were going to do things differently, only to go back to old habits after a while? New Year's resolutions are a perfect example of this; so many of us make them, but very few follow through. And that's because you are either not serious enough about your goals or there's no-one to support you.

Learn to see stress as a wonderful energy that can push you into the direction of your dreams. So the next time you feel stressed, say, "Oh-oh! I know this feeling, I've been here before! But rather than suffer this time, I will recognise what's happening and I will take five minutes to slow down and listen to my heart. For when I connect to my inner light, I will discover new ways to honour myself and my life."

There is nothing you have to do, there is nothing you have to achieve,
there is nothing you have to believe, there is nothing you have to prove,
and there is no-one you need to save.

But you have unbounded opportunities to do just that.
If you wanted to.
Because before, during and after life, you can decide how you wish to experience it.

6. "How can I let go of guilt?"

What would you say if I gave you ***one*** statement that can sort out your feelings of guilt once and for all? Wouldn't that be helpful? Especially if you are a sensitive person, it's good to have something to help you get rid of any unwanted guilt. So here we go: The next time you toss and turn over what you should or shouldn't have done or said, and you are serious about ***letting go*** of that annoying feeling, remember this: Only feel guilty when you do something with ***deliberate*** intent.

So, if you find yourself lying awake at night thinking, "I have upset this person, or I have caused that argument" I want you to ask yourself:

- "Was it my deliberate intention to upset that person?" If not, ***let it go!***
- "Was it my deliberate intention to cause that argument?" No? Then ***let it go!***

When I was about 20 years old, I used to be a terrible worrier. The smallest remark, comment, or suggestion from friends, teachers or colleagues, would be enough for me to bite all my nails and think that the whole world was against me. It was pathetic; I was aware of what was happening and that I was seeing things that weren't there, but I had no idea how to stop it. Then one day I heard someone talk on the radio about how to overcome guilt. That speaker, a very famous American author, Sylvia Browne, said, "Only feel guilty if you did something with deliberate intent." I think my life changed that day. It was amazing to me that such a basic statement could be so true. From that day onwards, as soon as the slightest feeling of guilt came to my mind, I immediately asked myself, "Hang on! Reality check! Did I do it on purpose or not?" And that's how I learned how to let go of guilt instantly, rather than letting it ruin my life.

We all feel anger sometimes; it is part of being human and thus part of the evolution of our soul. So if you have upset someone or caused trouble by speaking your mind, let it be. That's a natural situation that will sort itself out. When you have done something with deliberate intent, however, simply take responsibility for your actions and apologise. You might be surprised how easy it is to apologise to someone and to make things right. Moreover, it's a really good feeling, and it won't go unnoticed by the eyes of the Universe.

The more authentic you become and the more you respect yourself, the easier it is to let go of guilt. It will become easier to do the Guilt Reality Check: "Was it my intention to do ...... or not?" If not, you'll be able to let it go quickly. If yes, you'll be strong enough and proud enough with yourself to rectify the situation. And let me tell you, people will love you for being authentic and honest. Not only will they know who they're dealing with, but they will also learn from you, and your positive attitude will inspire them.

Now is a good time to reflect on some of the things that you feel guilty about. Let's do the simple Guilt Reality Check and deal with these unwanted thoughts once and for all. I want you to list all the things you feel guilty about. They can be things from the past, present and future.

Example 1: "I shouldn't go on holiday with my friends next week. My partner can't come along because he is at work. I feel guilty now that I have booked this trip."

Example 2: "My mother cried when I told her I had left my job and wanted to do something else; I have felt guilty ever since."

Example 3: "I feel guilty because sometimes I am too exhausted after work to visit my mother-in-law who's old and lonely."

Example 4: "I feel guilty that my business failed and that I have wasted the money people have invested in it."

Example 5: "I feel guilty because I cannot buy my children more of what they like."

Example 6: "I felt attracted to someone I was talking to at the party last night; now I feel guilty because I love my partner very much."

Example 7: "I feel guilty because I wasn't there when my mum died."

Part 1 of the exercise: Write down in your journal or below your own reasons why you experience guilt:

I feel guilty because:

____

____

____

____

____

____

____

____

____

____

____

____

____

____

Now for Part 2, I want you to carefully read all the reasons you have listed and honestly answer this question: "Was it my deliberate intention to create this outcome?" And as you do this, you will see that 99.9 percent of all the things you worry about so badly are invalid reasons for stress and guilt. And once you understand that it ***wasn't*** your intention to do wrong or to inflict pain onto someone, you will begin to feel so much lighter and better about yourself. It will be an enormous weight lifting off your shoulders. So, any time you feel guilty about things big or small, quickly do the Guilt Reality Check and be one step ahead of that annoying feeling. I discovered how to do this more than 10 years ago, and as a sensitive soul, it has changed my life. Now you can learn how to do it too!

7. "How can I improve my relationship?"

I would like to ask you a question: What do you expect from a relationship? Are you looking for meaningful companionship or simply a way not to be alone? What is it you are looking to "improve"? Finding some kind of deeper meaning or bringing back the spark are usually what people are referring to when they talk to me about improving their relationships. And that's perfectly understandable. Just think how fascinating it is when two souls come together and stay together for a long time; it's pretty amazing stuff. But there's a flipside to this golden coin: Unfortunately, too many people seem to change a lot as a person, either because being with someone makes them different somehow, or simply to keep the relationship going. And, of course, sooner or later, this will become problematic. When you change too much and you alter your beliefs, values or opinions, you are no longer being authentic. You are deviating from who you are as a soul, and that's not right. You can probably think of some friends who seem to have changed since they met their partners. Maybe you have tried to tell them that, but they will either not understand what you mean or tell you to mind your own business.

I am not denying that relationships require a little bit of "work" in terms of learning to listen, being patient, being more thoughtful, and so forth, but when you have to change your identity to the extent where you hardly recognise yourself anymore, you have a problem. Although you may love the one you're with very much, if you cannot be yourself and live the life you're meant to be living, then how much fun is left over for yourself?

If you really want to improve your relationships, talk openly about your issues and be lovingly assertive. If you wish to have a positive outcome, but feel you're not the best communicator, learn some new communication skills or methods like NLP (Neuro-linguistic programming) to help you create the desired outcome of the conversation.

Be respectful towards other people. We all have a unique soul and our own path to walk. Not everybody is on the spiritual path and not everyone is a sensitive soul, so be careful when you want to talk things through.

Spirituality is, once more, a great tool that can help us to better understand the subject of relationships. That's not to say that spiritual people don't have their fair share of relationship issues, but they usually deal with them a lot better, or at least quicker. Just consider that everybody on this planet is a soul that was born from the God Source and that we are all on a mission to contribute to the evolution of our soul. We experience a wonderful variety of things that can significantly help us with this task. Our soul learns from the loss of a job, poverty and extreme wealth, mental and physical ailments, and so forth. So just imagine how much it will learn from love and relationships! Heartbreaks, complications, arguments, betrayal, frustration, but also pure love, devotion and intimacy, are huge learning opportunities for your soul. Now that's where spirituality comes in handy: It helps you to understand why relationship issues show up in your life, but more importantly, why it's essential that you deal with them in the right way. And the right way is one in which both parties (and thus their souls) learn from the experience. Now you'll ask me, "What's the right way for me?" And I will, once again, refer you to your heart. Connect to your inner light and follow your intuition. What is your heart telling you to do? What does the challenge feel like? Does it feel like your soul wants you to learn patience, or maybe it's asking you to stand up for yourself and leave your relationship? When we are completely honest with ourselves, we usually know very well what the message is, but admitting it is a different story.

So, to come back to your original question of "How can I improve my relationship?" I suggest you listen to the truth that radiates from your heart and take it from there. And remember, the truth is never comfortable, but always helpful.

8. "How can I get more organised?"

Whenever I do a talk on coaching or spirituality, I always allow plenty of time for Q&A's with my audience. During one of those sessions a lady asked me what she could do to get more organised. That evening, I was hosting a talk about spirituality and so the question seemed a little bit out of place, but I was intrigued and obviously welcomed the question anyway.

In a nutshell, here is what I said: "What do you want to achieve, and what does being organised look like to you?" The lady didn't need to think long, saying, "I want to find a way to do more and become more efficient!" "Fair enough" I thought. "Let's use the spiritual life coaching approach."

I requested she took some time to spot the main reasons why she was not very organised. "I can't seem to motivate myself," she replied. She understood when I explained that tackling those reasons would be the key to becoming organised, but she told me that she's not motivated because "All my life, I've been disorganised, and it's made me feel like an underachiever." Bingo! The word ***underachiever*** stood out so clearly that I'm sure that everybody in the venue had noticed it.

I was so pleased she asked me that question, and I share it with you here because so many people want to be more organised in life, and feel lighter, but they are stuck. And there's no need for that.

If you feel that you are an underachiever and you tell that to yourself often enough, you will actually start believing it, which is, of course, very dangerous, as it affects your self-esteem. You will need to shift that belief if you want to become more organised, because I don't think you'll be very inspired to become organised if you see yourself as an underperformer in life—do you? That belief you hold about yourself is bound to distract you and slow you down. Good news, though, it is possible to change that belief and, with a bit of practice, you will soon become the organised person you've always wanted to be and you will feel in control again. Here are some tips that have worked miracles for both me and my clients. I also include specific examples that have worked for me when I wrote this book (finishing the book was my goal).

1. **Make things a lot easier on yourself: Set yourself achievable and measurable goals.**

Rather than having to write a certain number of pages, I decided to write about a certain topic every day. I broke my goal down into achievable chunks.

2. **Always make sure your goals are inspiring so that they keep you motivated.**

I loved seeing my first book coming together, and I was always motivated because all I had to do was write a little bit each day.

3. **Reward yourself for achieving your goals. Review what worked and why, and then apply this approach again the next time.**

I soon discovered that I worked best early mornings or late at night; that's when my inspiration seemed to flow the most. I learned to trust this flow and decided to go with it, rather than "making" myself work on my book in the afternoon, when my mind was preoccupied with other work. After I had finished the topics I wanted to write about, I would treat myself to small things like a nice cup of tea and a film or more important things such as contracting a designer for the cover of my book, which I was very excited about!

4. **Set yourself a goal beyond the goal.**

I swear by doing this, it helps me to get things done and be more organised. Let me explain: Whenever I prepare for a talk, the end goal is no longer simply the audience feeling happy and pleased that they attended; there's more.... As I am working on the content for my lecture, I already visualise myself enjoying talking to the people afterwards and listening to their personal stories and feedback they want to share with me. By setting a goal beyond the goal, I get extra motivation to do my very best and to make the talk as exciting as possible. Another example is the book you are reading now: Of course, getting my first book written, printed and published was a very inspiring goal, but what really drove me was the idea of doing talks based on the book afterwards! Again, a goal beyond a goal was enough to keep me on track!

9. *"How can I get better at decision making?"*

Should I leave my partner? Should I find another job? Do I follow my dreams? Do I set up that business? Should I invest my money? Do I tell my friends about my sexual preference? Should I buy a house or rent a flat? Do I join a gym, or should I pay for painting classes instead?

Making decisions, big or small, can be a real cause of stress. The "should I's" and "do I's" seem to take over our lives. This is especially the case in today's world, where pressure from society is high and so much is expected from us all the time. We all want to make the right choices, at the smallest risk.

But how can you know what the right choice is until you have experienced the outcome? So much of your time and energy is wasted on making the "right" decisions in life. It gives you stress, makes you anxious, keeps you up all night, and can even make you ill. It can also become dangerous when fake psychics, for example, capitalise on your insecurity to deprive you of your last penny.

Rather than giving your power (and money) away to other people, why not use your own wonderful guidance system to help you make the decisions that are right for ***you?*** By connecting to your inner light, you consult a wealth of wisdom that's already present within you. Now dare to trust that guidance and let it point you in the right direction. Ask yourself good coaching questions, such as "What will the cost be of not following my instinct?" and "What will be the benefit and reward when I ***do*** trust my inner guidance?"

Making decisions and hoping that they are the right ones is a part of life; it's very simple. They will show up and you'll have to make them. Some will be bigger than others, but all are important in their own right. So, would it not be useful to get better at making them?

Whether you take a calculated risk or you connect to your inner light, if the outcome of your decision is not what you expected, don't panic. Be gentle on yourself. You won't always be able to make the right decisions, so take the feedback and simply view it as a learning opportunity.

The stronger you become as a person, the easier it will be to make decisions and not feel upset if they turn out to be the "wrong" ones. There are no wrong decisions. Every experience you gain in life, good and bad, is of tremendous spiritual value. Granted, the bad experiences are probably not going to make you very happy, but you will learn from them in more ways than you realise.

I always share this advice in my lectures and personal coaching sessions: When your heart is telling you to make a decision, ***go for it.*** If your heart is telling you to wait, wait. Sometimes standing still is the best move you can make. But please stop being so hard on yourself and wasting your valuable time trying to make the right decisions.

Your life is like a jigsaw puzzle: Sometimes a certain piece comes our way and we don't know where to place it. Does that mean we are going to throw it away? Of course not! The best thing to do is to put it to one side and use it for later. Trust that your life's puzzle is coming together nicely, even though it may not always feel that way or you think the other pieces of your puzzle will never come to you. They will. In the meantime, be creative with the pieces you do have.

10. "I've heard people talking about 'bad karma'. What is it exactly and could this be the reason why so many things go wrong in my life?"

It might surprise you to see this question in the "Top 10" but you have no idea how many people seem to believe that their life is somehow "cursed". They have heard, read or seen something about the concept of "karma" and now fear that this karma thing is the reason behind all the things that seemingly go "wrong" in their life. I plan on writing an entire book on the topic of karma in the near future, but for now I would like to use this opportunity to give you a concise and practical explanation of what karma is and how it affects your life. I am sure this will help you put things into perspective and see how karma is something to be amazed at rather than afraid of.

Karma literally means 'action' and comes from the ancient language of India, Sanskrit. I like to see karma as ***experience*** and you could say that it is the "software of the soul". It contains both the blueprint of what you will experience during your life here on Earth and, maybe more importantly, the ***possibilities*** to create those experiences you wish to encounter during your lifetime. In other words, not everything is set in stone.

You may wonder who decides your karma for you. As we have explored in this book, you were introduced to the idea that you, being an eternal soul, are born from the God Source and therefore you are, indeed, a part of that God Source. Both God and you (being a part of God) wish to evolve your essence by experiencing life in many shapes and forms in many different places. Over the course of many lifetimes (and yes, YOU choose how often you want to return) you ***expand*** your karma. Sometimes this means you will want to gain certain new experiences during your life, such as being extremely wealthy, famous or physically challenged. However, your karma can also expand as a ***result*** of taking responsibility for an action you experienced in this or a previous lifetime. This is where karma plays a role. It is the ***universal law of cause and effect***. In other words, it could be that you ***caused*** something to happen, either in a previous life or in this one, and you are now experiencing the ***effect*** of that. People often refer to this as "What goes around comes around", usually to express their disapproval or disappointment about something, but it can also be a positive thing. There are still many cultures who believe that misfortune is some kind of ***punishment*** from "God". Of course people are entitled to their own beliefs, but when religion brings you fear rather than joy, I wonder how useful it is in terms of your spiritual growth.

The law of cause and effect isn't about "payback time" but gives you (read: your soul) an opportunity to experience both sides of the story. During your soul's evolution you have a chance to experience as many different things as you wish. There is nothing you have to do. There is nothing expected from you. But if you did decide to experience X-Y-Z in your life before you were born, then you might as well maximise the opportunity to do it ***this*** lifetime around, in my humble opinion. But even that is totally up to you.

I should probably also mention that it will be ***you*** and no-one else who will "judge" how well you've lived your life when you return Home. Your soul will reflect upon how you've utilised your life's opportunities to fill in pieces of the karma you chose for yourself. Depending on that ***realisation***, your soul will revisit some of the challenges that weren't explored or simply continue its evolution. It's almost like a child moving through the years at school: sometimes it may be appropriate to repeat a year, but that doesn't make the child a "bad" child.

When I talk to people about the basics of karma, they often ask: "So how much say do I have in my life? If everything was decided before I was even born, am I just playing a role?" Let me keep the answer as simple as possible to reassure you: you are ***not*** a slave to your karma. And you ***do*** have a huge say on what will happen to you in your life.

First of all it was you, no-one else, who decided upon the main experiences you are going to come across during your lifetime. Secondly, understanding the basics of karma really does give you a vital ***key to conscious living***, i.e. living a life with an increased awareness of what goes on in your life and why it goes on. It helps you to make sense of all the things that seem to go "wrong" for you: now that you know it might have been your very own decision to experience these challenges, would you still view them as "wrong"?

Understanding the dynamics of your karma will also allow you to "speed up" your karma by taking ***responsibility***. For example, whenever I am presented with a big challenge in my own life (and what most people would call a "bad" situation), I ask the Universe to empower me to take responsibility and help me face my challenge head-on. I ***know*** the reason why the difficult situation occurred in my life, whether it was in my life's blueprint or I somehow manifested it through my thoughts and actions, and so it takes me a ***fraction*** of the time to overcome the challenge and move on. It's almost like hitting the ground "hard and fast" and then getting on with things. It keeps amazing me how much this ***works***, and I hope from the bottom of my heart you'll find it helpful too.

There's not much fun or use in sitting in the corner complaining about how "bad" your life is once you understand that it's **you** who wanted to experience it that way. Yes, this also applies to more drastic situations as well. Allow me to share a very personal experience with you: I was abused at the age of 10 by a man in his late thirties. Despite the unacceptable behaviour from this man and the predicament I was in, I can now ***accept*** this experience for what it was and how both my soul, and his soul, fulfilled a part of our karma (victim and abuser). This works in a very similar way for people who have been the "victim" of any form of attack or accident. Now please don't get me wrong, I am not saying that those experiences are nice for people, or their friends and families, to go through. What I am saying, however, is that dealing with these challenges in a more constructive manner will allow everyone involved to ***move on*** more quickly. This is yet another massive advantage of practical spirituality and living consciously.

So, in truth, there is no such thing as bad karma. There can't be. Karma is what it is: karma.

Helping people to understand concepts like these, and thus creating a much lighter life, is something which gives me a tremendous sense of joy... and hence is an important part of my karma in this life!

Welcome Changes

I hope you have benefited from reading the tips I have shared with you in this book. They are drawn from my own personal experiences and my work with clients over the years.

The common denominator in all coaching work is about facilitating change. Different people have different goals, but they all have one thing in common: a desire for change. Whether it's finding a new job, making the right career move, discovering one's life purpose, building confidence, becoming a better communicator, attracting the perfect partner, or creating financial freedom, it is the strong desire for a positive change in their life that inspires people to call on the expertise of professional coaches.

But there is also another type of change that people may need a little help with from time to time. This category can be called ***unwanted change,*** such as an unexpected breakup, being made redundant, losing a friend, or a failed business venture. These changes are often very hard to deal with and can be traumatic experiences.

And then there are the changes that I help people with that I find very fulfilling. These changes occur when people slowly but surely grow to become the person they really want to be. They realise that their current circumstances prevent them from spreading their wings and that something will have to change in order to live their life to the full.

During this time of transition, a good coaching conversation will help people to explore the different possibilities and bring the support, guidance and understanding that are needed. With newly gained insight and a calmer mind, people quickly find the direction that's right for them.

How to Deal with Change

There are two ways of dealing with change: You can resist it (and spend a lot of valuable time and energy), or you can do what I always invite people to do; ***embrace*** change and really use it as an opportunity to do things you would never have considered doing otherwise. To help my clients better understand the process of change, I often ask them to visualise a large hourglass. The sand passes from one large reservoir to another, but it can only reach the second reservoir by going through a narrow passage. We can compare that narrow passage to the changes we are facing. We are often pushed and squeezed into ways that make us feel uncomfortable, but the quickest way to get out of that situation is by going with the flow and embracing the changes, not fighting them. Moving on in life and raising your game will sometimes present you with challenging situations. But when you connect to your inner light and follow the guidance from your heart, I guarantee that you will be strong and confident enough to make the choices that are right for you. And as you learn how to do that, you will begin to love yourself even more for being strong and authentic.

No pyramid was ever built in a single day. Consistent effort, passion and devotion put one building block after the next into place. Appreciate the changes in your life as learning opportunities to finally become a happier person. Make a conscious decision to take your life to the next level and enjoy it all the way. Remember that you are a part of the Universe and your soul decided to experience life here on Earth through you. Understanding that gives you everything you need to enjoy your journey, with all its good and challenging aspects. You made a conscious choice to live this particular life now, and it presents you with great opportunities to experience it fully. Explore the pathways of your soul, and use your God-given power to create the reality of your dreams. Not all of life is set in stone, and there is so much room for manoeuvring. Yes, you experience life here on this planet (and other places) for the evolution of your soul, but no, not everything is predestined. Certain people, certain circumstances, certain events, certain means, and certain ideas will show up in your life, and we humans will call them "good" or "bad". But they are merely like the dots in a children's book that need connecting to reveal the image. How fast you connect those dots is up to you. Occasionally some dots will be missing and you'll need to be creative and add your own.

The more consciously you connect all the dots that appear in your life, the more you will recognise the pattern, and in time be amazed by the magnificent design your soul has in mind for you.

I sincerely hope the tips and guidance in this book will help you on your exciting journey.

Embrace the changes; they will be extraordinary.

Much love,

Christoph Spiessens

Spiritual Summary: Revisiting the Main Tips (and more!) for Personal and Spiritual Growth

- Define what you want from life
- Express your gratitude every day
- Tell people how much they mean to you
- Believe in yourself
- Use positive affirmations
- Keep fit
- Stop all negative thinking
- Be gentle with yourself
- Hug people
- Commune with nature
- Always see the beauty of the moment
- Never put yourself down, even jokingly
- Join local and international support groups
- Do at least one nice thing for yourself every day
- Watch children play
- Smile often
- Join a class in holistic healing
- Slow down when talking
- Sit quietly for two minutes every day
- Imagine your "wings" growing stronger as you get ready for your day
- Make a list of qualities that make you so special
- Visualise your aura reaching out to people
- Listen to the voice within
- Stop saying "yes" when your heart is saying "no"

- Stop saying "no" when your heart is saying "yes"
- Think back to what you wanted to become when you were a child
- Travel, study and expand your horizons
- Express your creativity in ways that feel good to you
- Say "Thank you for a safe journey" when you get in your car
- Eat healthy food
- Respect others and appreciate that they are entitled to their beliefs
- Calm your mind
- Organise a charity event for like-minded spiritual people
- Spend more time on your hobbies
- Try a holistic therapy
- Don't manipulate people
- Use Post-it sticky notes with positives statements, and put them in your office or kitchen or on your bathroom mirror
- Sing!
- Avoid watching or listening to the news
- Tell your friends about your interests in spirituality
- Create a website or leaflet so that people know what you do
- Make more time for yourself
- Explore your sexual desires
- Surround yourself with white light
- Look at the stars
- Contact a spiritual coach to help you develop your spiritual side
- Drinks lots of water
- Let go of friends and people who hurt you
- Write about what spirituality means to you
- When you wake up, thank the Universe for being safe and protected
- Be authentic
- Get plenty of sleep
- Only help those who want to be helped
- Watch nature documentaries
- Review your values and beliefs—have they changed?
- Love yourself and others will follow you

- Refuse abuse in any shape or form
- Slow down
- Listen to people who inspire you
- Attend a workshop on spiritual development
- Be a healer
- Try to understand the meaning of your dreams
- Know that the way you look makes you unique
- Ask people what they value about you most
- Use positive feedback to do more of what you do well
- Respect your body
- Listen to self-improvement CDs
- Welcome help from the realm of Spirit
- No-one controls your thoughts but you
- Avoid goals that put you under pressure
- Be more playful
- Respect yourself
- Make sure there's a balance in giving and receiving
- Be your own life coach
- Use your power wisely
- Say "Thank you" when you turn off the radio
- Surround yourself with people who like you
- Use your thoughts to create feelings of happiness
- Create a treasure box in which you keep special objects
- Forgive yourself
- Learn how to meditate
- Create a sacred space in your home, just for you
- Listen to uplifting music
- Tell plants and flowers that you are grateful for their beauty
- Laugh often
- Appreciate that you are here to evolve your soul
- Reward yourself often
- Love your life and its challenges
- Ask for help; don't struggle unnecessarily

- Focus on that which inspires and motivates you
- Before you fall asleep, think of what you have learned during the day
- Join a gym and participate in classes
- Praise yourself
- Visit a bookshop or library
- Be excited about being a spiritual person
- Stop beating yourself up
- Tell yourself "I love you" often
- Dance!
- Make time for your friends
- Be in job that helps you grow as a person
- Be friendly to people from different age groups
- Try something new!
- Allow others to treat you well
- Be less defensive
- Buy yourself flowers
- Get a pet
- Spend time in nature
- Look after your grooming
- Be open to love
- Book yourself in for a massage
- Follow your dreams or they will follow you
- Congratulate yourself, even for the smallest things you do
- Ask the Universe for help
- Trust that the Universe knows what's good for you
- Know when enough is enough and then draw the line
- Use empowering, positive and loving words
- Give a compliment to at least one person every day
- Lovingly stand up for what you believe in
- Welcome changes

About the Author

Christoph Spiessens is the founder and director of Ankh Mind Body Spirit Centre, an innovative spiritual organisation based in Manchester, England. He is a sought-after spiritual coach and speaker, and works with clients worldwide.

He graduated as a Certified Coach at Coach Training Alliance in the United States, one of the top 10 life coaching institutes in the world according to Who's Who in Coaching, and recognised by the International Coach Federation. He also has a diploma in Successful Life Coaching and holds a Professional Certificate of Merit in Positive Anxiety Management.

Through his passion for practical spirituality he helps people connect to their inner light. He shows people how to use their inner wisdom to deal better with life's challenges and to find real happiness.

Christoph is a regular guest speaker at spiritual events and writes monthly columns for various lifestyle magazines. He was born near Antwerp in Belgium, and has lived and worked in London and Japan, before moving to the North of England in 2004.

For more information about Christoph, his coaching services, life-changing workshops and speaking engagements around the world, please visit his websites:

www.christophspiessens.com **www.ankhcentre.com**

Feeling Inspired?

Now is a good time to connect to YOUR inner light!

If you would like to:

- Find some help putting the tips explained in this book into practice
- Book Christoph Spiessens to appear live at your event
- Have more information about coaching sessions

Please visit www.ChristophSpiessens.com

For more information about **Ankh Mind Body Spirit Centre Ltd.** please visit www.ankhcentre.com or email: info@ankhcentre.com

It's your Life, your Future, your Turn.

To order this book online, please visit

www.connectingtoyourinnerlight.com

What I have learnt from this book.

1. Get more rest!!!
2. Learn to look after myself **ALOT** more.
3. Put myself a bit more b4 others.
4. Make more time for myself.
5. Don't take any abuse - cos - I don't have too - it's my choice & **MY** life. they destroy
6. Value myself a lot more.
7. Not listen to Track (5) depressing!
8. Be stronger - more assertive. Say **No** or I'm very sorry but **NOT TONIGHT** I'm Busy
9. Be happy with myself & accept me for what I am and what I'm not!
10. I'm lucky to have met a brilliant life coach to make me realise that I have so much inner light but did not know how & was so confused & lost to use it. But feeling it starting to get some energy. Cos feeling better about myself

starting to smile a lot more, even feeling radiant some days.. & strong. not so drained & looking pale..

(11) Starting to feel lucky that I exsist... first time since I was 22. I only ever got that feeling b4 and I remember the place, the moment & the time!!! I just got my dream job in the sun, in a uniform and helping people be happy! A Holiday rep!! & when I got that feeling I was in my manager's car on the way to the airport, he was training me @ the time.

(12). This book has reminded me how to feel like that again & how to find that feeling of satisfaction in my life. but with much more life experience & traumas & that I thankfully have overcome. & dealt with it, although flight residue still there!

Rosedale.Dench@gmail.com.

Kathryn Dench. orangatang&.